QUICK AS THOUGHT HE SEIZED A BRAND FROM THE FIRE AND THRUST
IT AMONG THE WOLVES (*page* 172)

RIVERSIDE BOOKSHELF

JUAN AND JUANITA

BY
FRANCES COURTENAY BAYLOR

WITH ILLUSTRATIONS
By GUSTAF TENGGREN

BOSTON AND NEW YORK
HOUGHTON MIFFLIN COMPANY
The Riverside Press Cambridge
1926

The Riverside Press
CAMBRIDGE · MASSACHUSETTS
PRINTED IN THE U.S.A.

THIS LITTLE STORY

IS AFFECTIONATELY DEDICATED

TO ALL DEAR CHILDREN EVERYWHERE

BY

THE AUTHOR

PREFACE

THIS story of two unfortunate fortunates —
mice let us say, seized by a tiger and escaping
from under his very claws — is true in its essen-
tial facts. That is, two Mexican children were
really captured some years since on the other side
of the Rio Grande by the Indians, and carried off
to the Llanos Estacados. After four years spent
in captivity, they made their escape, and safely
accomplished the almost impossible and truly
incredible feat of walking three hundred miles
and more through virgin wilds, with only such
protection as Una had, and no friendly bull like
Europa's to shorten so much as one weary mile
of all that great distance, led no doubt by guardian angels who knew enough of mundane geography to bring them first to the frontier of Texas,
and then restore them to their mother in Mexico.

F. C. B.

ELMWOOD, *May* 7, 1887

CONTENTS

ILLUSTRATIONS

JUAN AND JUANITA

.·.

CHAPTER I

THE TIGER SPRINGS

ABOUT twenty years ago there was not a happier family in all Mexico than one living near the village of Santa Rosa, province of Coahuila, and consisting of a *ranchero*, his wife Anita, and their two children, Juan and Juanita.

They had a great deal to be grateful for and to enjoy; a comfortable home, large flocks and herds — which constitute the wealth of that country — health, work, and, best of all, a tender love for one another. They had a great deal of another thing, some of which they could very well have spared — name.

The father called himself Don José Maria Cruz de las Santas,[1] prided himself upon his pure Castilian lineage, and was never tired talking of his '*sangre azul*,' or 'blue blood,' and his superiority to 'the ordinary Mexicans.'

His wife had no aristocratic pretensions what-

[1] Pronounced in English: Hosay Mareea Croos day las Santas.

ever, and, instead of always talking about the
past, was content to do her duty in the present.
She was a simple and rather ignorant woman, but
so well did she apply herself to her home duties,
that never had any man a truer, better wife,
children a more passionately devoted, self-
sacrificing mother, nor house a more capable
mistress than the Señora Anita. If she had a
fault, it was that she was altogether too unselfish,
and she would willingly have worked herself to
death for those she loved.

And there was enough to do; for, although
Don José was reckoned a rich man, he lived as
simply in most respects as his poorer neighbors,
and never seemed to think of spending his money
on servants, carriages, fine clothes, and the like
luxuries. Fortunately he was not too fine a
gentleman to work, in spite of his excessive
vanity about the Cruz de las Santas, whose re-
nown he honestly thought filled the world. On
the contrary, he diligently herded his own sheep,
sheared them in season, branded his cattle,
trained his horses, and did other outdoor work,
and he naturally expected the Señora Anita to be
equally industrious. Nor was he disappointed;
for when she was not making *tamales*, or *tortil-*

las,[1] she was sprinkling and sweeping the floors
and courtyard, or bringing in great earthen jars of
water, or spreading out the family linen to bleach
in the sun, or training the rebellious tendrils of
the grapevine that covered one side of the house
and supplied them with immense bunches of
delicious Paras grapes at one season of the year
— in short, doing something for the good of the
household.

And no matter where she went, she was always
followed by Juan and Juanita, who trotted after
her from morning until night, yet always felt
themselves welcome, and no more in the way
than did the chickens they saw under this or that
hen's wing when they went out to feed the
poultry that swarmed about the place. If his
mother seized Juan when he ran up to her with
the crown of his broad *sombrero* heaped full of
eggs, it was to draw him to her side and stroke
his hair, and praise him for having found them.
Or, if Juanita tumbled into the brook near which
the Señora was washing in laborious Mexican fashion, the garment, whatever it was, was
dropped, and soon the dripping little figure was
being pressed against her loving heart, while

[1] Mexican dishes.

the tenderest articulate and inarticulate cries of sympathy and affection were poured out on the unfortunate, and so much love shone in the mother's soft, brown eyes that it was worth any child's while to get a wetting in order to see it there and hear the caressing, '*Mi alma! Mi vida!*' ('My soul! My life!') that came so musically from the Señora's lips.

Busy as she was, the Señora found time to do a great deal of 'mothering,' and her children lived always in the sunshine, indoors and out, as joyous and volatile as the butterflies they chased, as brown as the berries they sought, forever leaping and dancing like the brook in which they were forever wading, the happiest of created things. They did not deserve much credit for being happy, for, except in the golden age of the world, there were never two children who had more to interest and amuse them, and less to vex them. Their few tasks came properly under the head of pleasures; they had no lessons to learn, only a few simple rules to obey; no fine clothes to soil or spoil; and as for playfellows, they had each other, the pigeons, chickens, lambs, kids, ducks, puppies, and other young things about the place, not to mention the birds, frogs, squir-

rels, and one especially sagacious and long-
suffering shepherd-dog, Amigo, their most faithful friend and constant companion. They were so
happy and so busy that it did not often occur to
them to be naughty; but if they did get into
trouble, it was always Don José who punished
them and the Señora who made them sorry for
what they had done. As soon as she dared do so,
she would go to them, take them in her arms,
murmur, softly, '*Pobre desgraciado!*' ('Poor disgraced one!') or '*Niña mia!*' ('My little girl!')
pour balm into all their wounds, take all the
sting and the bitterness out of their sore hearts,
and so lead them out, chastened and mild, to
kneel at their father's feet and beg forgiveness;
and then she sent them out to play, and smiled as
she heard their shouts and laughter.

Their home, or *hacienda*, was not in the least
like any house that you have ever seen, most
likely. It was roughly but strongly built of stout
pickets driven firmly into the earth near enough
together to allow the space between to be daubed
with clay and thatched with *tule*, a long reed
that grows in the Mexican country wherever
there.is standing water. Inside there were no
carpets, curtains, mirrors, pictures, or books,

and only a little furniture of the simplest kind; but, though homely, it was homelike, which is not always the case with far finer houses. The floor was only the earth enclosed, but much tramping and the Señora's endless sweepings, and brisk use of a watering-pot with which she laid the dust twice a day had made it quite smooth and hard. The ceiling was festooned with long strings of jerked beef and onions, and red peppers — the latter a prominent ingredient in everything the Señora cooked, and so much relished by Don José that it was his habit to pull off a handful at odd times and eat them as we would grapes or figs, although they would certainly have choked any one who was unaccustomed to the luxury.

Perhaps, among other distinguished peculiarities, the Maria Cruz de las Santas family had been made fireproof, and so could indulge in dainties that would have proved fatal to ordinary people; perhaps Don José had carried his insensibility to burning liquids and vegetables by a long course of Spartan banquets, and would himself have been blown up early in his career by one of the dozen peppers with which he now seasoned every meal. However that may be, it really seemed as though he could swallow molten lead without winking. A spoonful of those tiny live-coals called *chiles* disappeared down his throat without bringing the least additional tinge of color into his sallow cheek or the suspicion of tears to his eyes; he always took his coffee boiling; and as for the catsups and sauces that we call hot and serve with soup or fish, it is my belief that he would have mistaken them for ices if they had come in his way.

Everything within the *hacienda* was kept in a tidy state by the Señora, the few cooking-utensils bright and clean, the family effects disposed in an orderly fashion about the room, the walls of which were whitewashed regularly twice a year. So good a housewife was sure to have some place to store precious things, and accordingly in one corner there were some rude shelves where small packages of coffee and sugar, dried fruit, and what not were kept; and it was a spot that interested Juan and his sister more than any other, for here were always to be seen one or more tall pyramids of a confection called *peloncillos* [1] wrapped in golden straw. How their eyes did glisten, to be sure, and their mouths water when

[1] Pronounced pay-lone-cilyos.

the Señora got one down, slowly unpacked it, and then broke off a piece and divided it between them! This was almost sure to happen on Sundays, the days of their saints, the *fiestas* of the Annunciation and Assumption and all the great festivals, on San Miguel's day, San Antonio's day, and whenever they were supposed to deserve the treat. There was nothing they liked better, not even loaves of the fine Mexican bread known as *pan de gloria*, which they enjoyed equally in the baking and the eating. It was a blissful performance to watch the Señora get out her materials, deftly fashion each little cake in turn, make the sign of the cross on it, and pop it into the oven; it was still more delightful to see them taken out, so hot, brown, delicious! and to be given as many as two hands could hold, and to run off to the garden with them! So good a woman as the Señora could hardly be lacking in piety; every morning and evening she was wont to kneel in humble, fervent prayer, with little Juan on one side and Juanita on the other, repeating after her their *pater-nosters*. And if the children were not made to study history and geography and arithmetic, like most young Americans, they at least had before them constantly the example of their sweet mother, and so got by heart, in the best way possible, the first and greatest of all lessons — love to God and man.

Near the house, on one side, was the *corral*, or pen for the sheep, with the shepherd-dogs guarding it like so many trusty sentinels. On the other was the Señora's garden, where she had lovely flowers growing or blooming always, great bushes studded with oleander blossoms, clambering vines of jessamine or morning-glory, cacti, aloes, and dwarf palms. Some of the children's most delightful hours were passed in this sunny, fragrant spot, rolling about on the ground with Amigo, caressing their mother's tiny Chihuahua dogs Chula and Preciosa, making wreaths to fling about their necks, or playing hide-and-seek behind the oleanders, while the Señora industriously clipped, watered, shaded or smoked the plants, planted or gathered seeds, or daily plucked immense bouquets which a prodigal nature daily replaced. Her work done, she would often sit down on the steps of a rickety porch attached to that end of the house where shade and a breeze were nearly always to be found; the children and the little dogs would swarm somehow into her lap; and there she would fondle and caress them all with that wealth of soft labials which the Spanish language possesses, or sing in a high, sweet, but, it must be confessed, very nasal, voice, song after song; in some of which, such as '*El Sueño*,' '*Mañanitas Allegras*,' '*Si yo te amo*,' [1] the children would join.

And now I come to the one cloud in the beautiful blue of that heaven on earth — a cloud that sometimes appeared a mere speck for months together, and so far away that it was almost lost sight of, and then suddenly grew black and terrible, and threatened to overspread the whole sky and work the most dreadful ruin and desolation. It needed but a look at the *hacienda* to tell the whole story; for all along its walls at regular intervals were holes through which to fire upon an attacking party, and the house and outlying buildings were enclosed in a picket-fence, with gaps here and there, intended to serve the same good end. The haunting terror, the curse of the country, was that it was liable to be overrun at any time by the Indians, who would sweep down upon it from their distant strongholds in the mountains, steal all the cattle

[1] 'The Dream,' 'Happy Mornings,' 'If I love thee.'

and sheep they could find, and murder the peaceful inhabitants, men, women, and children, or else carry them off into a captivity so horrible that it was dreaded more than death. The Mexicans, when they had any warning of the approach of the savages, would hastily drive their flocks and herds into the *corrals*, the poorer neighbors seeking shelter and protection from the richer; but it often happened that they were taken wholly by surprise, and then terrible scenes ensued. Every *hacienda* was for the time converted into a fortress, always well provisioned, in expectation of these forays, and so well defended that the Indians, who were not prepared to lay regular siege to it with artillery, scaling-ladders, battering-rams, or any of the appliances of civilized warfare, and who could not wait to starve the garrison out, were generally repulsed after a few fierce assaults.

At the time of which I write there had been no Indian raids for fully eighteen months, and a feeling of perfect security had gradually grown up. The flocks were growing larger and larger, and were every day driven farther and farther from the *jacals* [1] and *haciendas* in search of fresh

[1] Sheep-huts; pronounced hah-cals.

pasture. Don José heard in Santa Rosa that all
the Indians had been chased out of Mexico,
never to return, and he spread the good news far
and wide. Even the timid Señora Anita breathed
freely at last; she no longer made herself unhappy when her children (as children will)
strayed out into the surrounding country and
did not come back until late, and she even formed
the habit of sending them every day to carry
their father's dinner to him wherever he might
be. It was a great weight lifted from her mind and
heart, and never had she been busier or happier.
It was true that they sometimes heard vaguely
of Indian depredations in Texas; but that was
not Mexico; and was not everybody quite sure
that all danger was over?

But one bright, beautiful summer day, when
all the world looked so lovely that there seemed
to be no room for trouble or sorrow in it, a terrible thing happened that overwhelmed not only
the Las Santas family, but many another, in
grief unutterable.

It came in this way. The day opened with a
gorgeous sunrise, with splendid tints of rose and
gold, which the Señora lingered to admire as she
walked back to the house from the well in the

fresh coolness of the early morning, carrying on
her head a huge *olla*,[1] so nicely poised that not a
drop of its contents brimmed over. As much
could not be said for Juan and Juanita, who,
with smaller jugs, tried to imitate her example;
for, instead of following their mother and making
at least an attempt to achieve the same graceful,
erect, smooth way of gliding over the ground,
they ran on ahead, and kept turning and twisting
their heads and looking back at her, which caused
small streams of water to pour down their backs
or laughing faces, while the Señora made a mild
pretence of scolding them, and really rejoiced in
their beauty, health, and happiness. The sun
itself, now fully revealed, was not as cheerful a
sight to her as her two merry, lovely children, and
she watched all their movements with fondest
pride and delight. Breakfast over, the gate of
the courtyard was thrown open, and through it
the long procession of lowing, hooking, trampling
cattle pushed themselves and one another out
into the open, followed by an immense flock of
sheep and goats trotting meekly, bleating pitifully, running awkwardly to right or left in
timorous battalions as the herders cut at them

[1] Earthen jar; pronounced o-yah.

with their long whips, or as Don José's vicious little mustang bolted in among them, and, feeling a pair of enormous rowels driven into its sensitive sides, bolted out again. The gates were then shut again and made fast, and those who were left behind at the *hacienda* settled down to the usual peaceful and monotonously regular duties of the day.

The Señora first made some preserves, and then betook herself to a favorite employment, the manufacture of the beautiful Mexican blankets, which is one of the great industries of the country. She had many difficulties to contend with in making them. Her only loom was a row of wooden pegs driven in the walls, her spinning-wheel was almost as primitive, the wool from her sheep of but an indifferent quality; but such were her energy and womanly skill that she somehow contrived to clean, card, spin, and dye very beautiful yarns, brilliant of hue, unfading, and of many shades. Of these she made, from designs of her own, handsome, durable, waterproof blankets, that, in spite of all the local competition, fetched a third more than any others in the market of Santa Rosa when she chose to sell them, which was not often. On that particular morning she finished putting in the warp and woof of a *serape*[1] for Don José, and, having filled her large shuttle with yarn, went hopefully to work upon the border as though it was to be the work of a day, instead of a year, thrusting the shuttle patiently in and out, in and out, between the threads with her slender, supple, brown fingers, and singing '*Mañanitas Allegras*' more through her nose than ever.

When she saw by her clock (the broad band of sunshine streaming in at the door) that it was high noon, she put by her weaving, got dinner, and, while the children were eating, put up Don José's midday repast in a rush basket and filled a gourd with fresh water. She presently despatched Juan and Juanita with these, following them to the door, and giving each a fond embrace as well as maternal counsels and cautions. She stood there watching them as they trotted briskly across the sun-baked courtyard, carrying the basket between them. Amigo, who had been taking life comfortably in the shade on the other side of the *hacienda*, dashed after them at the last moment. The Señora got a last glimpse of

---

[1] A blanket having in the centre a hole through which the wearer slips his head. The *serape* is worn by the Mexicans when they go abroad.

the children's laughing faces as they successively stooped and patted Amigo, looked back at her, and called out, *'Adios Mamacita!'* ('Good-bye, little mother!') *'Adios niños adorados!'* ('Good-bye, darlings!' [1]) she replied affectionately, and kissed her hand to them.

The gates closed on the outgoing trio.

The Señora went back to her dinner, and then settled down to her work, well content to have some hours of uninterrupted labor to give to the *serape*, which she intended should be the handsomest she had ever made — a birthday gift for her husband.

The children walked away westward across the sunburnt, rock-bound plain toward the place where they knew they should find their father and the flock. Whenever the basket got too heavy for them, they stopped; and they were by no means in such haste as to feel debarred from enjoying themselves. They picked many flowers on their leisurely way; they spent almost three quarters of an hour in watching and thwarting the innumerable companies of large red ants that were marching in long files across the country; and they applied themselves seriously to the

[1] Literally, 'Good-bye, adored children!'

work of thrusting their fingers into the large fissures made in the prairie by many parching months of excessive heat, and hollowing out a trench into which Amigo's tail could be neatly fitted and then covered with earth. This was a performance of which they never tired; and when he had stood enough of these attempts to raise him in the scale of animals by depriving him of his caudal appendage, he would get up suddenly, shake himself violently, as likely as not sending a small cloud of dust into their eyes, and stalk away good-humoredly, his only rebuke the dignified one of refusing to come back when called. It was not until Amigo had made this stand that the children realized how late it was growing, and when at last they came to the edge of the little thicket of mesquite trees, where Don José had sought refuge from the noonday glare, not all their voluble excuses saved them from a good scolding. Their father's vexation, like his appetite, was soon appeased, however. Juanita was soon allowed to light his pipe and to sit down in his lap, and Juan fell to playing with the cord of his father's immense *sombrero*, braided and coiled about the brim in imitation of a snake with its tail in its mouth, and then tried the hat on, saying

proudly, 'It is not *much* too big for me, is it,
Padre mio?' although it continually slipped down
over his black curls and laughing eyes. Once,
when this happened, Amigo growled and rose up
and began to nose about uneasily, but lay down
again when reproved by Don José, who said,
'That stupid dog doesn't know you.'

The day was still and sultry, and it seemed as
though all the world was holding its breath.
The scanty foliage of the mesquite shrubs was
motionless overhead. Nothing was to be seen
but the sunlit plain before them stretching away
to a semicircle of low, distant hills, a beautiful
little lake close by reflecting the flood of light
which poured down upon it, a few buzzards
soaring with the most exquisite grace and repose high in the blue intensity and immensity of
the Mexican sky. There was nothing to be heard
but an occasional bleat from the flock brought
to shade and water near the lake. A more perfectly tranquil, peaceful scene could not be
imagined.

Don José, having smoked, bethought himself of
his usual midday siesta, and sent the children
away; and, nothing loath, they ran off to play
under the trees with the kids and lambs, and to

feed the shepherd-dogs. This took some time, during which Don José slept profoundly, having laid aside his pistols and the heavy belt in which his knife was stuck, and propped his gun against a tree. For, although he had grown careless, as people who live in perilous times and places are apt to do whenever there seems no immediate danger of losing life or property, he never dreamed of leaving the *hacienda* without being well armed. Long immunity from Indian raids had effaced the anxiety he had sometimes felt about the safety of his wife and children, and for himself he had no fear; but, if only from sheer force of habit, he would no more have thought of leaving off his knife or pistols than his boots when he dressed himself in the morning.

When the children returned they found their father awake, refreshed, good-humored, and disposed to caress his little daughter, who perched again on his lap while he stroked her hair and admired its texture and abundance, her large dark eyes which looked up at him, and, above all, her fair skin, proof of the Castilian blood of which he was so proud.

'You are now six years old, are you not, Juanita *mia?*' he said.

'Yes, father mine. And Juan is eight,' she replied.

'In a year, so, like this,' said Don José, measuring with his hand a certain distance from the ground; 'in another, so — and so — and so — and so — and so,' the hand rising every time.

He went on talking of the days to come, when she should be big enough for this and that, and succeed one by one to the occupations and dignities of Mexican womanhood, while the children listened and laughed. But he was interrupted. The shepherd-dogs began barking furiously, and rushed into the *chaparral*.[1]

Don José sprang to his feet, armed himself, and seized his gun, thinking that wolves or the Mexican lion or leopard were attacking the flocks. The children nestled close to him, and he looked hesitatingly at them, reluctant to leave them. At that moment the sound of horses' feet and wild yells came to them from the direction of the lake, and they knew that the Comanches were upon them! It was a frightful moment, and the children were paralyzed by terror. But Don José, being an old woodsman, did not lose his presence of mind for one moment, though he

[1] Thick and brambly underbrush.

turned pale under the shock. 'Run! run to the *chaparral!* hide! fly!' he called out to the children in a voice of agonized earnestness; and, as they obeyed, he too ran, but toward the Indians, to divert their attention from Juan and Juanita.

He had not gone far when a loud scream from Juanita told him that his ruse had failed, and, turning, he rushed back again, to see that three Indians had come in from that side, where they had probably for some time been concealed and watching him.

They were so intent upon catching the children that they did not notice the return of the father until he fired on one of them and shot him through the heart. Don José then drew his pistol and began an attack on the other two, who were glad to take shelter behind trees from his well-directed fire. Taking advantage of their defeat, he seized a child by each hand and tried to gain the shelter of a dense thicket near by. But his success was only momentary, for fifteen or twenty Indians burst into the open ground and opened fire upon him. He soon fell, mortally wounded, but still cried out, 'Run! run!' with all the energy of his soul.

Disobeying him for the first time in her life,

Juanita would not leave him, but dropped down by him, threw her arms around his neck, and, hiding her face on his bosom, shrieked out her grief and terror; while poor Juan, who could not bear to leave either of them, added his cries to hers.

The Indians closed in around the little group, and now began one of those terrible scenes too common in both Mexico and Texas. At last even their hideous revenge was complete, and Juanita felt herself seized by the hair from the rear, and sank on her knees with a shriek of despair. The mother of the brave whom Don José had slain had determined to take what vengeance she could for his death, and began raining cruel blows on the trembling child at her feet. But this fresh calamity, instead of further subduing Juan's spirit, seemed to have the effect of arousing him from a horrible dream. The squaw's attack upon the little sister he loved so transported him with fury that, lost to every consideration of prudence or personal fear, he tore off a hard, dry mesquite limb from the nearest tree, and dealt the old Indian woman a series of blows on the head that came so fast and furious that she was forced to let Juanita go and give her whole attention to her enraged assailant.

She was a woman much above the ordinary stature, and with her painted face, black, snaky locks, and glittering eyes, she might have appalled an older and bolder enemy; but Juan was beside himself with rage, and his very size gave him an advantage, for he slipped from her grasp over and over again, dodged here and there, struck at her when she least expected it, and darted about her very much as a hornet might have done. The odds were so great, though, that the battle must have gone against Juan had he not been suddenly reënforced by Amigo, who, with a savage growl, leaped against the squaw with all his sharp teeth showing. Utterly infuriated, she drew her knife and made a fierce lunge at Juan, who swerved swiftly to the right, and replied with a blow that nearly stunned her. The Indians yelled their approval of his courage; and, just as she was about to spring upon him again like a tigress, one of the chiefs coming up, seized and held her firmly for a moment, shook her in reply to some fierce words that she muttered in her rage, and then pushed her down on the ground, where she lay panting and glaring at Juan.

The chief now announced that he should take

the children as his prizes, and forbade their being further injured, saying that Juan would make a *bravo soldado* (brave soldier), and should be received into their tribe, where he would take the place of the warrior they had lost. Don José's flock was then hastily gathered, and the Indians prepared to fly with their booty before the Mexicans could rally and pursue them. The children were taken up behind two Indians, and the whole party pushed rapidly across the plain to the hills, where they took the trail and began winding up the side of the mountain. Arrived at a certain high point, they halted and were joined by some Indians stationed there to look out for pursuers.

The spot commanded a beautiful view of the valley spread out at their feet, which was made more impressive by being enveloped in great part by the peculiar gloom of a fast-approaching storm, across which the late afternoon sun sent long, melancholy shafts of amber light as it reluctantly withdrew from a vain struggle with the powers of darkness. But there was no one to enjoy the scene.

The Indians exchanged a few words and nods and grunts, and then drove their heels into the flanks of their horses, impatient to get a night's start of possible avenging *rancheros*. The children, alarmed by the way the mustangs slipped about on the stony hillside, clung desperately to the Indians in front of them, speechless with fright and misery and exhaustion.

As they were about to move on again, Juanita looked down, and there, far below her in the distance, dimly seen in the waning light, was the *hacienda*. Her impulse was to throw herself from the horse as the first step toward reaching it, and she made some such movement, but was jerked back into place by her old enemy, the squaw. Her poor little heart was bursting with anguish. Holding out her arms toward the *hacienda* she broke into passionate sobs and a piteous cry, '*Mi madre! Mi madre!*' ('O my mother! my mother!')

The old squaw half turned and struck her.

The very clouds overhead could not stand the sight of so much wretchedness, and let fall a great shower of pitying tears, shutting out the last ray of sunlight from the world, and of hope from the hearts of two captive and despairing children.

CHAPTER II

BY THE WATERS OF BABYLON

How is it possible to paint the grief of the gentle, affectionate woman on whom the hand of God was so heavily laid! All that afternoon she sat working quickly and diligently with no presentiment of evil or danger to those she loved better than life itself. Once, it is true, a bird flew in the open door; and as the Mexicans, unlike the Romans, do not think the flight of birds a good omen, the Señora crossed herself and felt the chill of superstitious fear for a moment; but, having driven the intruding songster and unpleasant thought both away, she was soon singing again over her *serape*. It was many a long day before she sang again; for now first one neighbor and then another rushed in, ashy pale, terrified, incoherent, bringing ever more and more dreadful news, as the night came on, of her losses and theirs. Upon hearing that her husband had been killed, and that her children were missing, the poor soul gave one heart-rending scream, and, fainting, lay as one dead for so long that she was supposed at one time to have gone beyond the reach of sorrow. But at last the dark eyes opened again, and with memory came anguish unutterable.

The thought of the children caused her more poignant suffering, if possible, than the fate of her husband, although she had loved him and lamented him with ceaseless groans and tears. 'Where are they? Are they murdered too, and their precious bodies lying all mangled and defaced out there? Are they living and wandering about in the night and storm? Oh, tell me! Where are they? Oh, my children! my little ones!' she cried out to the circle of sympathizers gathered at the *hacienda*, as she paced backward and forward weeping and wringing her hands, or cast herself down on the floor in despair.

When daylight came it was she who, with old Santiago and one of the herders, went out into the country and looked everywhere for some trace of the children. But hours and hours of search revealed nothing except Juan's hat, which had fallen off in his encounter with the squaw. Early as it was Don José's body had been already taken up by the neighbors, who, with great kindness and delicacy, had spared her the pain of seeing him until they had prepared him for burial and rendered him a less horrible spectacle. And so, when the poor, distracted creature came back to her desolate home after her fruitless quest, it was to find a rigid figure lying in one corner of the *hacienda* and the good Padre Garcia from Santa Rosa waiting to see her, and a crowd of her simple tender-hearted country-women assembled who broke into lamentations, and exclamations, and tears with ready sympathy, when they saw her. And that afternoon it was borne away by a small cavalcade of horsemen into Santa Rosa, where it was buried in consecrated ground attached to the Church of the Conception. Padre Garcia said as many masses for the repose of his soul as though he had been the President of Mexico. A rude wooden cross was erected on the spot where he was killed; and, the claims of death on the community being satisfied, life was again taken up. The women who at first lingered about the Señora wishing to comfort her, were one by one reabsorbed in their own duties and interests, and dropped off from the *hacienda*. And it was just as well, for they had not the power, although they had the will, to help her. For one thing they were all agreed — that Juan and Juanita had either been killed, or would be in the course of a few days, when the Indians should find them burdensome; and their idea of duty was to discourage the Señora from talking of either husband or children — to convince her that there was nothing to be hoped.

It was natural that, in the absence of proof to the contrary, she should cling to the belief that they were still alive. And this she did in spite of their well-founded arguments and assertions; but secretly, for she had not the heart to oppose them. It was only to her especial friend Martina da Castro that she expressed the conviction that had come to her in a certain way, and that never wholly left her in the years that followed, although she had many a day of deepest depression when the hope could only be known from despair by its tormenting lack of certainty. 'It was the day after the interment of my husband,' she said, 'and all was black, black within me. There was but one thought. Where were my children, on earth or in heaven? I felt that I must know, and who could help me? Who but she that was also a mother, the Blessed Virgin.

And I thought, "she knows what she felt when she lost her son for but a day! She will not leave me ignorant. I will ask her." And I fell on my knees, and said fifty Hail Marys and five Our Fathers, and vowed all the candles for the high altar, and a *burro* for Padre Garcia who is getting lame, and asked that I might only know were they alive or dead. And I don't know how long it was after I had stopped praying with my lips, but as true as that I speak to you I heard a voice saying, "They are alive! Be comforted." And I opened my eyes, and just then the sun burst out from under a cloud and shone about me, and it seemed to me that it was the Madonna's hair and veil I saw before me for a moment, just as I see you sitting there smoking. And then it went, and I thanked her for answering me, and got up, and ever since I have known it; my children are still alive.'

'*Es posible — Es posible*,' replied Martina, half impressed by what she heard, half reluctant to destroy such a comforting illusion.

And so the days went by for the Señora, days of sad endurance, patient toil. For some things she had no heart. The *serape* remained unfinished. The flowers, uncared for, bloomed and spread, or withered and died as the case might be, so that the once pretty garden was soon the most neglected and forlorn spot about the place, overgrown with weeds, parched by the sun, deserted by the Señora whose faith was not equal to keeping it up for the sake of her children. She believed them to be living, indeed, but she had not been told that she should see them again, she sadly thought, though she could no more help hoping it, and living it in imagination, than she could help breathing. The sight of the children's pets was always a stab to her loving heart, but these she did not neglect. When a bird flew in at the door now she thought, 'Ah! you cannot hurt me now,' and did not drive it away.

There were no songs now in the *hacienda*, but every moment of waking thought with the Señora was an inarticulate prayer for Juan and Juanita. Of the boy it comforted her to remember that he was strong, active, courageous. If he was in captivity with the Indians he would not suffer as a delicate child would have done. He might even shield and protect his little sister. At thought of her Juanita, so young, timid, helpless, the Señora's eyes always overflowed, no matter how often it came; and that it came very often, bringing a troop of other sad thoughts in its train, her tear-dimmed eyes and the deep lines of her sad face sufficiently attested.

The neighbors got quite tired of seeing a face that grew ever sadder and sadder; and, finding themselves unable to dispel a melancholy as profound as it was patient, left her very much to herself. Some of them went farther and set before her the sinfulness of grieving so much. Others made it clear that great punishments always came close upon the heels of great sins. Even Martina, the tender-hearted and sympathetic, begged her earnestly to give up the foolish idea she had taken up of seeing her children again, when she must know now that they were dead and in paradise with their father. She had known it always; and, for her part, had often prayed for the repose of their souls. The Madonna and all the saints would be greatly displeased by such a want of resignation.

To all this the Señora, who could neither recall her terrible sins nor forget her terrible sorrows, had but one reply — deep sighs, looks of unspeakable weariness, tears that were ever rising, but not often shed.

'You are very obstinate,' said Martina, at last;

'your silence does not deceive me! You still believe the *niños* are living.'

'*Si, Si! Es verdad,*' confessed the Señora, humbly.

'Then, if they are alive, where are they? Why haven't they come back? Respond. Tell me — you,' said Martina severely.

'God knows! God protect them!' cried the Señora, and fell to weeping passionately.

As for the *rancheros* that had followed the Indians, they soon returned.

The pursuit of Comanches by Mexicans at any time is very like that of a hawk by a canary; but when to their genius for predatory incursions, their bold, unexpected attack, paralyzing blows, and swift retreat, the Indians add the advantage of twelve hours' start in flight, one might as well expect to overtake a thunderbolt. When the *rancheros* were clattering over the stony streets of Santa Rosa in the early morning, the Indians felt themselves already out of danger, and were leisurely taking their way toward the Rio Grande with the intention of crossing it and going up to the head-waters of the Colorado, in northern Texas, their *pied-à-terre* — one hesitates to say home, a word full of sacred and civilized associa-

tions having little in common with the mountain
lair in which these savages spent the intervals between their murderous forays. But, like Issachar,
these wandering tribes know where to crouch as
well as when to spring, and there is no more beautiful country than that lying between the two
great rivers, the Brazos and the Colorado, where
they enter the Llanos Estacados — a country of
bold cañons and lovely valleys abounding in game,
bears, deer, turkeys, antelopes; with wild bees
swarming in every rocky cliff, and feeding upon
the wild plum, which blooms there in great
variety of color and size, or the wild grape, which
perfumes the air for miles with its delicate, delicious odor. Near one of the many clear lakes
that industrious beavers have created through-
out that region, a tranquil sheet of water overshadowed by tall cottonwood trees and graceful
willows, with silvery many-tailed fish leaping,
gliding, winding in its cool depths, the Comanches came at last to a full halt, after a journey
that had sorely tried their little captives. The
horses, cattle, and sheep they had stolen were
turned out to pasture, as were the jaded animals
they had ridden. There was nothing to do now
but to eat, sleep, rest, and get ready for another
raid on the frontier settlements.

They arrived at night, and the children, half-dead with fatigue, were taken to the lodge of their protector, old Shaneco, where they at once dropped off into a sleep of profound exhaustion that lasted ten hours. When Juanita opened her eyes next morning, she was quite dazed, and could not at first make out where she was. The first object that she saw was a familiar one. It was Amigo, who had spent the night curled up at her head, and now advancing, with a tail all wagging friendliness, poked his cold nose into her face and began to lick her right cheek. Juanita pushed him away and sat up rubbing her eyes. She then began to look about her, and her glance wandered from Juan, who was near her, still asleep, to the skins stretched over poles, that formed the walls of the lodge, to Shaneco, snoring loudly opposite, a great heap of buckskin and blanket merely, apparently. Her mind was still lingering confusedly among these details when her eyes fell upon Shaneco's gun, and bow and quiver placed within easy reach of his hand, and then out upon the open space in front of the lodge, where a squaw was building a fire. In a flash the past came back to her, and she was throbbing with tumultuous emotions — love, grief, fear, despair.

But, young as she was, she had already learned a measure of self-control from the experience of the last few days, in which cries and tears had always been followed by blows, so she only shrank back into the corner again. As she sat there in dumb misery, not daring to move or speak, much less sob, she happened to look down, and there, withered, bereft of every petal, and stripped of every leaf, was the bare stalk of the osage-plume she had pinned securely in her dress the morning she left the *hacienda*, as she and Juan were walking over the prairie. This brought such a bitter memory of her mother, home, happiness, that the tears would come now, and she made noise enough to wake Juan, if not the chief, although she made several convulsive efforts at repression.

Juan put his arm about her and called her his '*querida hermanita*,' kissed and embraced her, and did all he could to soothe her, and even Amigo understood that something was wrong, thrust his rough head against her shoulder, looked up into her face and whined uneasily. The truth was that Amigo had had his misgivings from the first about this Comanche business. When the children were put upon the horses he perfectly comprehended that it was not the proper place for them, and barked furiously for a while. But, having put his disapproval of the proceeding on record, and finding that no one paid the slightest attention to his remonstrance, he very sensibly held his peace, and, during the journey that followed, trotted patiently in the wake of the company, determined, no doubt, to be the guardian and protector of Juan and Juanita, come what might.

The three friends were still comforting each other by love expressed as plainly in Amigo's eyes as by Juan's lips, and still caressing each other, when the squaw glanced in and saw them. She beckoned to the children to come outside. They obeyed; and, picking up a piece of wood, she pointed toward a thicket at a little distance, and made them understand that they were to go and get the fuel she needed. Not knowing that she wanted dry mesquite, they picked up the first branches they saw lying on the earth, and ran back with them; but, if they expected the praise and thanks that they always got when they rendered the Señora any trifling service, they were sadly undeceived. They received a kick apiece instead, and were sent back to repair what the squaw considered an unpardonable piece of stupidity, for the Comanches use mesquite alone for fires whenever it is to be had, partly because it makes a very hot fire, but chiefly because it yields so little smoke. In that pure, clear atmosphere smoke can be seen at a great distance, and would betray their whereabouts to their enemies, the whites, or to other Indian tribes with which they are constantly at war.

The children came back the second time with their arms full of mesquite, and were then given their first lesson in Comanche housekeeping, and taught how to build a fire *à l'Indien*, and this more by example than precept, for, although Mrs. Shaneco gave the most voluble directions all during the operation they could not, of course, understand a word that she said. What she did was this: First she went down on her knees and scooped out a small hole in the earth. In this she laid little short pieces of mesquite, piling them up sugar-loaf fashion, and adding a few more at a time as the first supply burnt out until the fire was as large and as hot as she thought desirable. The little Mexicans watched her with the interest children always feel in anything of the kind, and it was well that they paid strict attention to what was going on; for, after that morning, Shaneco's wife never condescended to so much as set the fire off with her flint-and-steel unpatented match-box, and any failure in this or in any other of the daily duties required of them was always severely punished.

Old Shaneco was never cruel to them, and was sometimes even kind, but his young wife was a shrew, and a hard taskmistress to two children who were accustomed to do very much what they pleased and had never known what it was to be harshly treated. They suffered so much, indeed, from the hardship of their new life and from homesickness and the utter want of any-thing like kindness or sympathy, that, if this had been all, they could not have been other than deeply unhappy; but when to this was added slavery, endless tasks, constant beatings, it is no wonder that they were utterly wretched and felt that they could not bear it.

The poor, foolish little rebels could think of no way but one out of their troubles, and that was to run away. They ran away, accordingly, and were of course almost immediately recaptured, and so dreadfully punished that they were in no hurry to repeat the experiment. The desire for freedom, the passionate longing to return home, remained, indeed, and strengthened as time went on; but they had been taught by their recent experience how completely they were in the power of their enemies, and dimly realized that they would have to be a good deal older, wiser, stronger, before they could cope successfully with them.

The image of the Señora, alone and ever sorrowful, never left the children, however, and, like her, they were constantly picturing to themselves a joyful reunion. They talked of it when they were alone, and together made their simple plans for bringing it about.

'I will learn all that I can from the Indians, and when we get big we will give them the slip, and if they overtake us I will kill four or five chiefs, and the others will get frightened and run away, and then I will take you to our mother, and say, "Here is Juanita, brought back to you,"' Juan would say with *naïf* braggadocio.

'And I will look everywhere for blackberries, and save them up to eat on the way. But you must wait until some time when Casteel is on the war-path. I am so afraid of Casteel,' Juanita would reply.

'I am not afraid of Casteel. If he fools with me I will run a spear in him, and shoot him, and cut off his head,' said Juan with more spirit than truth; for he was afraid of Casteel, only the encounter was an imaginary one, and, like his elders he naturally wished to make a good figure in it.

It has been seen though that Juan was a bold, courageous lad; and, happily, he was not long enough under the cruel rule of Shaneco's wife to lose this fine natural temper and develop into a timid, cowed creature, afraid of everything; for, in the second year of their captivity, she died, greatly to the relief of Shaneco as well as the children, for if ever Indian was henpecked it was that redoubtable warrior.

After this things went more smoothly at the lodge. Instead of being treated as captives, Juan and his sister were now made as much a part of the tribe as though they had been born in it, and Shaneco may be said to have directed their education, which, if different from that of civilized children, was far more valuable to our little Mexicans than any Paris or London could have afforded, as will appear later, and founded on sounder principles than those of many civilized parents and guardians, since it was admirably suited to their needs, and fitted these young savages perfectly for the life they were to lead. Truth to tell, Shaneco had gradually come to feel an interest in, and some affection for, the white-faced little girl, whose gentle, pretty ways, obedience, and youth disarmed hostility, and for the intelligent boy, who was so eager to learn all that he could teach, that it is a wonder that no suspicion of what was in Juan's mind ever entered his astute teacher's brain. The children were now much happier, and showed it, which doubtless gave him the idea that they were quite reconciled to the prospect of becoming Comanches, and had forgotten or would soon forget all about their old home.

And another thing that fastened the conviction that his plans for his little captives were succeeding was the sheer impossibility of their getting away. He knew, although the children did not, all the difficulties that would attend any attempt to reach the settlements, perils great enough to daunt the bravest man — a wilderness of three hundred miles to traverse; hunger, thirst, exposure, ending in almost certain death, either by starvation or violence from savage tribes, or wild beasts scarcely more savage. After the first futile effort at escape, with its unpleasant results, he thought they would submit to the inevitable, and, having learned to endure, would end by embracing the nomadic life. That two little children without horses, arms, or older companions, should dream of taking such a journey never occurred to him, and indeed, if they had been anything except children, and, as such, ignorant of its dangers and risks, they never would have entertained the idea for a moment. But, having come to them, it struck ever deeper and deeper roots until it became a fixed resolve; and, even when some of the difficulties of the undertaking became known to them, as they grew older, they refused to recognize them as insurmountable, and would not give up the long-cherished plan.

Even among his Indian playfellows Juan soon became conspicuous for his activity and endurance, his strength, courage, and skill, whether shown in running, leaping, swimming, wrestling, climbing, or in more serious occupations. Shaneco often felt proud of him, though he never said so, at least to Juan, who yet understood the grunt of approval and the gleam of warmth that

came in the cold eyes when he ran like a lizard up
to the very top of a fine cotton-wood, and then
dropped swiftly from branch to branch, until he
lightly sprang to earth and stood again by
Shaneco's side, radiant and breathless; or bor-
rowed the chief's bow and arrow for a moment,
and made a shot that would not have disgraced
any man in the tribe.

Naturally a manly lad, he took very kindly to
the hardy, open-air life, and had, besides, set
himself in earnest to excel, while Shaneco, seeing
only the result, not the motive, thought that
wisdom was justified of her children, and would
turn an 'I told you so!' glance upon Casteel, who
had been of the capturing party, and had been
opposed to taking any prisoners, was opposed to
the introduction of any foreign element into the
tribe, and would have knocked either of the
children on the head, as soon as fill his pipe, had
they not possessed a powerful protector. Many
a kick and cuff did he give them as it was, and
there was a restrained brutality in his manner to
them that quite subjugated Juanita and made
her tremble when she heard his step. It was
chiefly owing to his counsels and distrust that
Juan was never allowed to carry any weapon

except a toy bow and its arrows, with which, however, he practised incessantly, and became so expert that the more good-natured of the warriors willingly lent him their bows occasionally, taking care to keep an eye on him all the while.

A bow was indispensable to a warrior, and a good one considered equivalent in value to a well-trained war-horse. This may seem strange, but was owing to the fact that much time, trouble, and skilled labor go to the making of one. It fell to the lot of the old men of the tribe to make them; and, although they did nothing else, it was no sinecure. Juan was never tired of watching them at work upon them and took the keenest interest in the result obtained, until Casteel one day forbade his being permitted to look on and sent him to the right-about.

Mulberry wood was generally used for the bow, and the process of preparing it was a very tedious one, for it had to be slowly seasoned, and in the shade, to keep it from cracking open. When sufficiently dry and mellow it was repeatedly rubbed with rattlesnake-oil, and gradually worked into various shapes and lengths, the lower part being made the size of the arrow, and notched that it might be the more securely bound with sinew, the points having pieces of hoop-iron nicely and securely adjusted and filed as sharp as a knife-blade, the bow-string being made of sinew from the back of a deer or buffalo. Switch dogwood or wild china was used for the arrows. Bundles of the proper length being cut, tied in bunches, and seasoned, the bark was peeled off, and the arrows run between two rough sandstones having a half-circle cut out of each piece. By putting the arrow back and forth in this primitive turning-lathe it was gradually made perfectly smooth and round, and then had only to be pointed and feathered.

The more proficient Juan got with his toy bow the more discontented he grew with its limited capacities, and the more he longed for his ideal bow, which was one like Shaneco's, made of the best wood, without a flaw or knot in it, light, and strong as steel, yet elastic, with its quiver beautifully ornamented with beads and eagle-feathers and the claws of a lion and grizzly bear; full, moreover, of the best arrows, striped in gaudy colors, and prettily feathered with the feathers of the yellow-hammer. It was true that he had killed many a quail, rabbits, squirrels, and small game without end, and knocked the feathers out

of a wild turkey, but what was that compared
with what he could do if he only had a proper
bow? The very sight of Shaneco's filled him with
envious irritation. All his sport in the present
and hopes for the future depended on his getting
such a one, and it was a problem that he was
always trying to solve. He spent hours in thinking about it; sighed profoundly to think that he
had no war-horse to give in exchange for one;
knew that he had not the skill to make one, nor
the chance; begged for one repeatedly, only to
be invariably refused; despaired of getting one,
and was always pouring his woe and want, and
grievous disappointment into Juanita's sympathetic bosom.

'How am I ever to take you home with this
thing?' he would say, kicking his bow contemptuously away a yard or two.

'Sh! speak Spanish!' she replied, looking
anxiously around to see whether they were overheard. Both had rapidly picked up the Comanche tongue, and only reverted to their own
when they were alone. 'It is not such a bad bow.
I shot a rabbit with it this morning. And it is all
you have got,' she added.

'But don't I tell you that we shall be prisoners

forever, unless I can get a better?' he said, impatiently.

'Be patient, Juan; perhaps Shaneco will teach you how to make one, or give you one,' she said, to cheer him.

'No, no! That he never will,' he replied, disconsolately. 'What shall I do?'

And Juan was right. Shaneco taught him a great many things — how to snare quail or rabbits; how to fish and shoot; how to imitate the cry of wild turkeys; how to follow an enemy's trail and keep him from returning the compliment; how to travel by night from the stars, and by day from the sun and the moss growing on the trees, and much wood-craft, beside, but never let him have a bow such as he coveted — showed displeasure, finally, when urged to grant the request. There was nothing for it but to bide his time; and, afraid of rousing suspicion, Juan at last dropped the subject altogether, but was none the less resolved to get that bow.

The months were running away meanwhile, and the years. The Señora's heart was sick, indeed, with the pain of a hope that was dying day by day; but that she felt it would be death to relinquish altogether. 'No news! No news of my children!' was the thought that met her when she opened her eyes every morning, that tugged at her heartstrings all day, and did not always leave her when she lay down at night; for she often dreamed of wandering over the world in search of her lost darlings whom she could not find, and of whom she could hear nothing.

CHAPTER III

FREE AGAIN!

THE fourth year of their captivity found Juan and Juanita well-grown, strong children, perfectly healthy, as rough and tough as the cubs they had stolen from a bear, and almost equally wild and brown. If the consuming desire of their mother's heart could have been gratified, and she could have seen them, she would certainly never have recognized her fair, refined-looking children in the young barbarians who were hardly to be distinguished from their Indian playmates.

And if Don José (himself now an ancestor) ever looked down on the last representatives of the ancient Maria Cruz de las Santas family, he must have been shocked; indeed probably disputed their identity, and disowned them altogether. It was well that the Señora did not see them. She would have been afflicted by a thousand things to which they had grown quite accustomed, and had, indeed, ceased to regard as evils. Her children were now as dirty, as daring, as tattered and nondescript in costume, as well able to conjugate the two auxiliary verbs of the

Comanche as of the Russian tongue — to steal and to lie (*vide* a Russian writer) — as any Indian of them all, and were, consequently, in high favor with the tribe.

It is not wonderful that the little captives preserved but few of the habits and traditions of their country and family. The sign of the cross was all that remained of what they had learned, at their mother's knee, of religion, and this was only remembered when they were in great straits. Their Spanish was getting quite rusty from disuse. Gentleness and politeness were not *à la mode* in the society in which they found themselves, and, if only in self-defence, had to be abandoned. As for cleanliness, not only, as the ancients knew, is dirt 'a painless evil' to children, who, in this, are all natural savages, but if they had been ever so much inclined to be dainty, such refinements as baths, soap, brushes, were out of the question, and so the poor little Cruz de las Santas were not even 'ordinary Mexicans,' but most extraordinary ones.

One thing they had not lost, and that was their love for their mother. This was their salvation. Without it they would have become part and parcel of the tribe into which they had been adopted. The vine-clad *hacienda*, the garden, the flocks — all the features of their old life had grown misty and unreal, and they had become interested to a certain extent in their actual surroundings, and enjoyed the free, wild life they were leading. But, when most contented, the thought of their mother kept alive the wish to return to civilization; her sweet face and tender love were still clearly mirrored in their hearts and minds. They loved to talk of her, of what she had done and was doing, of her sadness and loneliness, and most of all of the joy that would be hers when they returned. Yet it is probable that they would have deferred any attempt to carry out this haunting vision for some time — perhaps in that time have lost all desire to carry it out — but for one of those occurrences that look on the surface like an accident.

Juan and Casteel, who had never been friends, got into a violent quarrel one day about some game that the former had shot and the latter had seized. It ended in Juan's getting a beating; and, on his complaining to Shaneco of his wrongs, he got no redress or satisfaction. This fanned Juan's latent dissatisfaction into a flame. Infuriated by Casteel's taunts and cruelty, and Shaneco's apparent indifference, which in reality was intended to make him duly submissive to his elders, and maintain tribal discipline, he lay awake all that night, indulging in the most revengeful, furious thoughts, and trying to make some plans for punishing his enemy. But with the morning light came enough soberness to show him the folly of pitting himself against Casteel; and, in the fit of disgust that followed, the memory of his mother's affection and indulgence naturally came back to him with redoubled force, and crystallized the fluctuating emotions and desires of the last few years into a fixed intention to make another effort to escape from the Comanches as soon as possible.

Having made this resolve, he was eager to communicate it to Juanita, who was overjoyed to hear it, and agreed to everything that he proposed. Innumerable conferences followed between them, and both began to prepare in earnest for the undertaking.

'Oh, if we only had horses!' she said to him one day when they had been discussing ways and means. 'We could gallop, and gallop, and gallop away so fast.'

'Horses! nonsense,' said Juan, who knew the

unerring certainty with which his foes would
take his trail, and, in a few hours at most, recapture them. 'Do you want to be —?' making
a swift circle about her head to indicate scalping.
'We must leave on foot, and at night. I don't
want horses; but I must have a bow, and I mean
to get one, Nita. I have thought of a plan. You
will see!'

In about a week Juan's preparations were
complete; and, going in search of his sister one
morning, he found her watching a game of hunt-
the-slipper, which, with certain variations and
additions, is extremely popular among the Indians, and played by old and young. On this
occasion two braves were absorbed in it, and
there was a ring of interested spectators looking
on. Eight moccasins were spread out on the
ground in front of a young warrior, who took a
bullet in his right hand and passed it swiftly
under the soles of the moccasins, above and
around them, until he contrived to drop it into
one unperceived. His opponent was then required to guess where it was. If he failed he
paid a forfeit; if he succeeded he gained the
stake.

Each had a pile of blankets, buffalo-robes, and

what not beside him, and they had been gambling for hours, while two old warriors squatted down near them, rattling dried peas in a gourd, and keeping up a droning chant that was utterly hideous and discordant.

When Juan joined the lookers-on, the situation was exciting, although no noisy demonstration showed that the Indians felt it to be such. A very handsome Mexican blanket was at stake, and Casteel was taking a good deal of time to consider the important question that would decide whether it should be his or not.

'Can't you see where it is? Where are your eyes, you bat?' said Juan tauntingly, after a long silence.

'Where is it, my fox? Tell me that, and you can take this, the best blanket I have,' Casteel scornfully replied, laying his hand on one that was partly visible under a buffalo-robe, and pulling it out in full view.

'It is under the flap of the third moccasin,' said Juan, whose quick eye had noticed a very slight bulge on the inside of that shoe, the nearest to Casteel, skilfully chosen by his adversary on the principle that the best place to conceal anything is immediately under the nose of the person who is looking for it. Casteel gave a most disdainful grunt, and, on hearing it, Juan stooped down and drew forth the bullet, saying, triumphantly, 'Here it is! Give me my blanket.'

The spectators shouted. Casteel drew his knife by way of reply, and the next moment Juan's knife also flashed in the sunlight. But this time Shaneco upheld Juan, made Casteel yield, gave the blanket in dispute to its owner, who seized Juanita by the arm and hurried her away to the wood.

'I have got a blanket now,' he said to her joyously, when they were out of ear-shot, 'and a flint and steel, and some punk to kindle our fires, and some fish-hooks, and a little corn, and a wallet of dried meat. I am all ready. What have you got?'

For answer Nita (as her family and we shall call her for convenience' sake) ran to a certain spot, tore away eagerly the leaves that apparently filled a hollow stump, and brought back quite a little supply of dried meat that she had saved, together with some nuts and other things that Juan rejected, after which they had a long talk in which it was settled that they should leave that night, just before midnight, when the moon

would be rising; that Juan was to keep awake
and give Nita the signal by laying his hand on
her face; and that once out of the Indian encampment they would travel southwest until
daylight, and then hide until night came again.

'I have found out where Mexico is,' said Juan.
'I pretended to Mazo [a playmate] that I thought
it was due north, and quarrelled with him about
it, and he told me not only the direction in which
it lies, but a great deal besides that he has heard
from the braves. Wasn't that sharp of me?
Don't you be frightened, Nita. I will take care
of you. You can just go to sleep to-night, and I
will call you when the time comes.'

The weather was warm and pleasant, and the
Indians were sleeping in the open without shelter
of any kind, so that it was not a question of
stealing away from Shaneco alone, but from all
the tribe. When Juan and Nita lay down as
usual, side by side, near their protector, they
were so excited that it seemed easy enough to
stay awake any number of hours, all night, indeed. But when two hours had gone by, in which
the tension of feeling had relaxed more and more
in the perfect stillness and quiet that prevailed,
little Nita's eyes would not stay open any longer,

and soon her soft, regular breathing told Juan that she was fast asleep.

He kept awake a long time after this, listening to every sound, wondering if the people about him were awake or asleep, thinking impatiently that the moon would never rise. From this his thoughts wandered to the journey he was about to take, and a thousand other things. Shaneco's huge figure got more and more indistinct, and a cricket chirped in his very ear now without rousing him. He was wandering over a wide, wide plain, he forded streams, he was lost in the woods, he fled from the Indians who were on his trail, whose wild yell sent him up into a sitting posture.

In short, he, too, slept; and when he could collect his senses he found that the yell of his troubled dream came from an owl that had perched in the tree above him, and given him the friendly warning he needed so much. He was about to get up, knowing that there was no time to be lost, when the voices of two or three Indians reached him and warned him to be cautious. They were talking and jesting about the owl, and it was quite half an hour before all was quiet again. Another time old Shaneco turned over, just as Juan was thinking of starting, and another interval of impatient waiting had to be endured.

At last it seemed to Juan that the moment had come. He had no difficulty about Juanita for the owl had aroused her too, and she was wide-awake, waiting for the signal agreed upon, in fear and trembling. Juan gently pressed her hand. They both sat up and looked about them. The camp was as quiet as the grave. Only the south wind gently rustled in the tree-tops, and carried a few dead leaves around in a minature whirlpool a few feet away. Every creature about them was wrapped in profound sleep.

After some moments of keen scrutiny of the dark forms dimly visible on all sides, Juan looked at Nita and pointed to the east where the stars were paling, and a faint, green flush admonished him to be off before a flood of golden light was poured upon every part of the valley. They quietly arose. Juan stepped lightly to the old chief's head, stretched out his hand, and took down the long-coveted bow and quiver. At last it was his! According to the Comanche code he was not doing anything disgraceful — behaving quite creditably, on the contrary. But all the same his naturally generous and affectionate nature made him feel some compunction when he glanced down at the unconscious Shaneco and remembered that he had always been kind to him. It would have been such an unmixed pleasure to steal Casteel's bow! A bow he must have, though, and what a beauty this one was, to be sure!

As he was about to move away with it, a lizard that had got into the quiver jumped down and scampered off across the grass. Shaneco muttered in his sleep, turned over on his back, and threw one arm up over his head. Juan was terribly frightened; but he had the presence of mind not to move or make any exclamation. He kept perfectly still and held his breath; but his heart beat so loudly that he thought it must betray him. As for Juanita, she shook like an aspen-leaf, but did not cry out or run away. After a moment Juan tipped noiselessly back again. Seeing his own bow and quiver at his feet, he picked them up and gave them to Juanita, who slung the bow around her neck. He then seized his wallet, and picked his way carefully between the sleeping warriors that surrounded them, she following.

When they were nearly out of camp, he took

her cold, little hand in his to reassure her. Just then a warrior coughed, and both started as though they had been shot. But nothing came of it, and they were soon skirting the wood where all their councils of war had been held, taking advantage of the dark shadows it cast in some places, and noticing that the tops of the trees alone were now glistening in the moonlight, which meant that it was very late, and that they must make all possible haste. As they scurried along in the uncertain light, they fully realized that they had deliberately defied one of the most warlike and merciless tribes that this continent has ever had in all its length and breadth; and as Juanita looked back fearfully over her shoulder from time to time, she imagined that she saw pursuers in every bush and tree, and even urged Juan to go back before their flight was discovered.

But once outside the camp his courage rose, and he stoutly refused to do anything of the kind. He took his bearings by the stars, and resolutely set his face toward Mexico, talking as boldly and cheerfully as he could all the while.

'Do you see that large beautiful star in front of you, Nita?' he said. 'We shall always travel toward it, for that way lies our home. Our mother is there waiting for us, and we must go to her, no matter how far it is, or how many moons it will take us. Are you still trembling? You mustn't be such a coward. We have got a good start, and, by the time they find out that we have run away, we shall be far, far away, and they will not overtake us. And if they do, I will not let them hurt you.'

Juanita was not particularly reassured, but said nothing, and they walked on rapidly in silence for some time. The wind blew fresh and sweet full in their faces, the moon had slowly died out of the clear heavens, and in the east the light had deepened gradually until all the sky was a miracle of ethereal loveliness. If the fugitives looked often at it, it was with no appreciation of its exquisite tints of rose and gold, but because the day of probable discovery and recapture seemed to be coming all too fast. They had been travelling about an hour, and, urged alike by love and fear, had put considerable distance between themselves and the camp. Juanita was even beginning to feel hopeful, when suddenly they heard a dog bark. It sounded so near that they thought the Indians were already upon them, and in a dreadful fright took to their heels and ran like lapwings for miles, indeed until, from sheer exhaustion, they were obliged to stop. Even in this race for life Juan did not forget one of old Shaneco's lessons; whenever he could do so, he chose the dry, rocky bed of a creek, in order that his trail might be lost, or only found with great difficulty after much loss of time. At last, panting and quite spent, they stopped to get their breath, encouraged to do so by the thought that they had outrun or baffled their pursuers.

As soon as possible Juan pushed on to a range of low hills, from one of which he began to reconnoitre his position. He saw in the distance a valley through which ran two dark lines made by live-oak and elm trees. The one that led off to the south followed the course of a large creek, which he knew lay in his way, and had been on the lookout for; so he cheerily explained to Nita that he knew exactly where he was, and that he should make a bee-line for the creek, where they could rest and hide themselves until the following night. Very soon after this they came upon a small creek, and had not to wait until they got to the larger one for a drink, for they had followed it but a short distance when they spied a deep water-hole. Eager to quench their thirst, they raced up to it, stooped down, and began to drink, but were again startled by a loud barking and howling, and some noise as to which they were uncertain, so close to them as to renew all their terrors for a moment. The next instant Juan distinguished the howling of a gang of coyotes, which was answered by a loud chorus of gobbles from the turkeys roosting, as usual, in the trees above the water.

Great was their relief; but these sounds reminded them that they must press on, being sure indications of the approach of day. The imperative necessity of finding some hiding-place forbade their resting, and they hurried on down the bed of the stream, walking altogether on the stones until they got to the place where it intersected the main, or Hunters' Creek, when they turned into that. The coyote concert still continued, and to the turkey chorus were rapidly added other sounds, such as the hooting of owls, the twitter of other birds, the chirp of insects. Possessed more and more by fear of their pursuers, as the sun rose higher and higher, the children ran on with all their speed, glancing to the right and left as they went, to see if they could find a place that seemed likely to shelter them, two desperate, hunted creatures.

Finally Juan came to a spot where a little brook emptied into the main creek, and there, a few hundred yards distant, was an immense oak tree in full leaf, its friendly limbs stretching out far and wide, and dropping low as if eager to offer them an asylum. Juan had never so much as heard of the royal fugitive who once fled to the heart of an oak for shelter; but he had often hidden in one for amusement, and he now turned into the brook, ran up the bank, clambered up on the lowest limb, gave Nita his hand to help her up, and was soon ensconced in a fork, or rather juncture of several large limbs with the main trunk, which he made more comfortable by wrenching off some small limbs and branches that were dead, and improvising a sort of rustic sofa. Now, at least, they could draw a long breath, completely concealed, as they knew themselves to be, by a dense foliage, in comparative safety. Only comparative, for they knew the wonderfully trained sight of their enemies would soon give them some clue as to the direction of their flight, and that they would be tracked with all the cunning and almost supernatural sagacity which the Indians possess.

They strained their eyes and ears for a long while after this, looking and listening, but saw nothing, heard only the gentle susurrus of the leaves about them, the gobble of a turkey, the howl of a coyote. They were very tired, but dared not go to sleep; talked little, and that in whispers.

While thus awaiting further developments, they had the pleasure of assisting at a *matinée musicale* of a novel kind, to which no one is ever invited, and which a hunter thinks himself lucky to attend (in a latticed box made by under-growth) once or twice in a lifetime. This was one of the coyote concerts of which I have spoken, and a droll performance it was, although conducted with great formality and deliberation. Juan and Nita, being concealed from view, had the full benefit of it.

About twenty wolves constituted the troupe, and were soon grouped on the sward beneath them. When the proper time came, their leader gave out one low, sad note, as if to command at-tention, very much as the leader of an orchestra raises his baton and looks around at the musicians under his authority. Then the other wolves gathered about him in a circle, but all facing him.

Then one wolf opened with a tenor howl of most piercing quality, and was joined in regular succession by the basso, contralto, soprano, alto, baritone, and so on until the whole pack was in full cry, each performer giving his whole mind apparently to his own score, and all keeping time by jumping up and down on their four feet with their noses lifted high in the air. This last was doubtless a mute expression of the opinion each artist had of his neighbor's performance, and increases the likeness of the whole to our musical entertainments.

These were familiar strains to Juan and Juanita; but it was one thing to hear them in an Indian camp and quite another out in the woods. Nita grew pale when she heard the unearthly long-drawn howls of the wolves below her answered by a prolonged wailing note from a gaunt old lobos in the distance. 'Only hear them, Juan! They are like demons in purgatory,' she said, and shrank close to her brother's side. They had the satisfaction of seeing the pack slink off as soon as they had gone through the programme for the occasion, and now the fatigue and excitement they had undergone began to make itself felt. The relaxation of the moment, their weariness, the soft murmur of the rustling leaves about them — all combined to make them drowsy, and, finally, both children fell asleep.

They were awakened by a well-known voice that filled them with dread, for they could not but believe they had been followed and their hiding-place discovered. And so it had been; but by a dear and faithful friend, instead of a cruel enemy — in short, Amigo! Missing them in the early dawn, he had taken their trail, unobserved by the Indians, and had unerringly followed them to the foot of that oak. Puzzled by the sudden end of the trail, he began to whine and gave a few short barks and a great fright to the children. He knew that they could not be far off, but where?

As for them, when they found that he had organized an independent search of his own, they were delighted; for they had been feeling very lonely and desolate, and that honest, loving face was a cordial to their hearts, and seemed to bring them fresh hope and strength. The next moment came the thought that if he were to begin barking again, it would certainly attract the attention of the Indians, if any were in the neighborhood. Juan parted the leaves, looked down, and

spoke to Amigo in a low, stern voice; and if ever
a dog laughed from Mother Hubbard's time until
now, Amigo did when he saw those two faces;
for Nita was visible also. It is certain that he
showed every tooth in his head and wagged his
tail most vigorously.

'It will not do to stay here now,' said Juan.
'We must leave this at once. Amigo would betray us, and they will look first along the princi-
pal water-courses. We must get over on that
ridge.'

So saying, he dropped to the ground, followed
by Nita. They could hardly control Amigo's joy
at seeing them again on *terra firma;* but Juan
quieted him, and the trio started off briskly for
the high land, which they gained, and from which
they had an extensive view. Long and anxiously
did they gaze across the plain to see if they could
discover any signs of pursuers. For a long while
they saw none, and rejoiced accordingly; but at
last Juan's sharp eyes made out some moving
objects on the distant hills — mere specks.

'Buffalo, wild cattle, or Indians,' he said,
putting the worst supposition last, in mercy to
Nita, whose teeth were chattering already in a
nervous chill. 'We must put some thickets be-

tween us. Come on!' exclaimed Juan; and, starting off at a run, he fairly flew over the ground, Nita keeping up with him astonishingly for some time, and Amigo frisking cheerfully ahead, as if out on a pleasure excursion of some kind.

Nita gave out first, and, stopping short, she burst into tears, exclaiming piteously:

'Oh, we shall be taken! We shall be killed! Oh, why did we ever run away?'

Impatient as Juan was to go on, he, too, stopped and did his best to console and animate her, and his kindness and affection had a great effect upon her. The sun was now high in the heavens; its heat added another distressing element to their flight, and they were, moreover, suffering from hunger and thirst.

'There, there, don't cry, *hermanita mia*,' said Juan. 'A few minutes won't matter. We will stop and get our dinner, and then we shall be able to travel for hours again. This way.'

So saying, he turned off to the right and made for the creek again. The season had been a very dry one, and he knew there was no water to be had except in the large streams, and there only in standing pools that were either fed by permanent springs from the bottom, or too deep to be affected by droughts. A cool, nice drink is always to be had from these if you understand how to get it; for, even when the water on the surface is so hot as to be sickening, by putting a canteen on a long pole and running it down quickly to the bottom, where the sun's rays can't penetrate, you can bring up a deliciously cool draught.

The Indians use vessels made from the skins of wild animals for carrying water, oil, and honey, and nature has provided them with an admirable substitute for canteens in the Mexican gourd, with its two globes connected by a long, narrow neck; when a halter is put around this, it is easily swung over a saddle-bow. It is a curious fact that these are found only in the countries where they are most needed, and, if planted elsewhere, degenerate into the common gourd.

Our runaways had recourse to mother-wit in the absence of both gourds and canteens. Juan had approached the water very carefully, avoiding footprints on the sand, and all other places that could betray him, and, kneeling down by the deep, still pool, he fell to running his hands down into it as far as possible, and throwing the water up towards the top, thus creating a current from the bottom, that soon gave them a fairly cool and most refreshing drink. He had taken pains not to spill any water, and had carried Amigo in his arms over certain patches of ground where the marks of his feet would have enlightened the Comanches. When they had all fully slaked their thirst, Juan led his little band on up the bed of the creek, intending to take them back to the hills again, and let them rest a little and eat something.

This move was not made a moment too soon. They had only passed the main trail that ran up and down the creek a short distance, when they heard the sound of horses' feet, and soon after voices. Now, indeed, they knew that they were in great peril; for they had been told that if they ever attempted to escape again, and were captured, they would be killed. Juanita fell into an ague at this crisis, but managed to keep up with Juan, who darted on up the creek, panting out at intervals, 'We must be out of sight before they get to the crossing.'

They had scarcely reached a hiding-place before the Indians rode down into the bed of the creek. There were fifteen of them, all armed with bows and arrows and lances. They were about four hundred yards away, and, Juan could see, had stopped, either to hold a council, or because they had made some discoveries. They soon determined what course to pursue. Eight of them rode up the bank. Four rode down the creek, and how Juan's heart leaped into his mouth when he saw the other three turn their horses' heads up the creek, Casteel's painted, malignant face coming first! Fortunately, he was not only a courageous lad, but had the peculiar order of bravery that gets cooler and more collected in time of great danger, and is full of inspiration and expedient. He did not lose his head in the least. Nita had fallen on her knees, crossed herself, and was repeating under her breath such prayers as came to her, consisting chiefly of agonized exclamations, 'O Holy Mother of God! O Jesus! save us!' Amigo was crouched down beside her, and seemed to understand the gravity of the situation and Juan's sternly whispered command to be quiet. Juan, as he peeped between the bushes, was a living incarnation of two senses, sight and hearing. They had been so hard-pressed that they had sheltered themselves behind the first clump of bushes they could find; but Juan knew that they were only partly hidden, and only safe until the Indians turned the bend of the creek and came in full view of their covert, when Casteel's keen eyes would be sure to penetrate the scattering foliage that intervened.

Desperate maladies require desperate treatment. Juan gave a swift glance to right and left, saw that the curve of the bend was a long one, heard that the Indians were walking their horses, and took a bold resolution. 'Come!' he said, suddenly, to Nita, and to her terror and amazement ran out of his hiding-place, and sprang again into the bed of the stream, in front of, as it were, in the very teeth of his pursuers! Whatever noise they made was drowned by the horses' feet. The banks of the stream were high enough to hide them from sight.

On they sped. Juan knew that a break in the bank, a trampled weed, a stone freshly displaced, a footprint, the slightest appearance of anything unusual would be detected; and detection meant death. But he did not lose his self-possession. Luckily the rock beneath his feet told no tales, though it echoed and reëchoed the sound of the horses' hoofs in such an alarming way that it seemed to Nita's excited imagination as if they must be ridden down every moment.

At last Juan saw with joy what he wanted, and instantly took advantage of it. It was an old tree that had probably been undermined by some freshet, and was now lying prostrate. He ran like a squirrel on it up to the top of the bank. Nita followed; and, if you believe me, Amigo did not let so much as one paw touch the earth. The three disappeared in the undergrowth beyond, leaving not a trace behind, just as the Indians made the turn that would have proved so fatal to them. Obeying a natural impulse the children ran swiftly away from the creek for a few minutes, and then Juan caught Nita's arms and bade her stop. She was glad enough to do so, for she was utterly spent and terrified nearly out of her wits.

'It won't do to leave the river bottom; we may run upon the other party if we try to gain the post-oak woods,' said Juan. 'We must keep still awhile and let Casteel's party go on.'

Gradually the sound of horses' feet died away. The children had become a little composed and a little rested after their race for life. They began to hope they were safe, and Nita's face had lost its ashy look, when their fears were all revived by a loud yell from the Indians who had ridden down to the mouth of the creek, and had there discovered some trifling proof that the children had been there.

Casteel's party heard this yell, and, turning, galloped back to join them. Juan knew that they would soon all be working at the trail together, like so many bloodhounds; but that, thanks to his precautions, it would take them some little time to find it. The instant his ear, which was laid to the earth, told him that Casteel had passed by, he was off like an arrow from his own bow in the opposite direction, with his little company close behind him, and did not stop until they had put five or six miles between them and their pursuers.

'Look at the shadows. It lacks only an hour of sunset,' he said joyfully on starting.

At first he kept in the river-bottom; but when the twilight came, he struck across the open country and gained the woods into which he and Nita plunged with inexpressible thankfulness, and, climbing again into an oak, were again quite lost to sight.

CHAPTER IV

ADIOS, SHANECO! ADIOS TODOS!

WHEN the strain of the day's alarms and exertions was over, and succeeded by darkness, stillness, and a temporary safety, poor little Nita got quite hysterical, and sobbed herself to sleep on Juan's shoulder. She refused to eat anything, and was the weariest, most footsore, entirely exhausted child that can be imagined; and but for the protecting arm that encircled her, the confidence that Juan's cleverness and daring had inspired, and her belief that they were to stay where they were for some time, she would have been utterly miserable. As it was, Juan had to scold her a little for being so sure that they would never see their mother again, and certain that they would eventually be recaptured. He told her that she must expect to undergo a great deal of hardship; that she must be brave; that he had a capital idea that would put the Indians off the scent; and, finally, that she must go to sleep. He made a hearty meal from the wallet, and threw down something now and then to Amigo who had stretched him-

self out at the foot of the tree, and deserved
to feast after his admirable conduct that day.
'A sensible dog, that; not once did he bark after
the Indians appeared, and only gave one growl
in the thicket. I hushed him up; but I thought
he would break out again. I believe he knows as
much as I do about it,' was Juan's last thought
before he, too, dropped off to sleep.

Amigo's whines awakened him at daylight,
indeed, before, and he was not sorry; for, after
the fatigue he had undergone the previous day,
he would certainly have slept late — a dangerous
indulgence under the circumstances. He roused
Nita, who awoke greatly refreshed and much
more cheerful. She was quite ready for breakfast now, and all the party ate with immense
relish of what the wallet afforded. 'It is lucky
that I held on to this yesterday, in spite of the
way we were chased. We should have had
nothing to eat otherwise. Now, Nita, this is
what I am going to do. I am going to travel due
south instead of southwest, all to-day, to puzzle
the Indians, who will be sure that I am travelling
toward Mexico. Let us be off at once,' said
Juan.

Nita looked wistfully at him, and would have

greatly preferred to stay where she was. Juan understood the glance, and replied to it, 'They would have you in two hours at latest,' said he.

On hearing this, Nita lost no time in getting down from her perch, and they set off. She was so sore and stiff that at first she could hardly walk; but that disappeared in a great measure as they walked on. They were not yet 'out of the woods,' and did not dare to feel too glad until they knew whether their foes had kept and followed up their trail. But the rest and food they had got, the exercise they were taking in the freshness of a fine summer morning, invigorated them wonderfully, and they marched along with great briskness and hopefulness, actually indulging in a joke occasionally. They faced south, and Juan picked out a mountain from which he could get a good view of possible pursuers, and perhaps find water.

It seemed to him only about three miles distant, thanks to the extraordinary purity of the atmosphere of that region, but proved to be about six. A long walk it seemed under a burning midday sun, and when they got to the mountain there was still the ascent to be made; for, as soon as they had come within sight of the woods that covered it, Juan's eyes had eagerly roved from spot to spot, until they came to one near the top, where the trees were a dark, rich green that contrasted decidedly with those about them. 'There is water, unfailing water!' he exclaimed delightedly. 'But you are dreadfully tired, Nita. You must have a good rest under that large oak before you begin to climb the mountain. We will take that ravine there, and follow it up.' They were both dreadfully tired and consumed with thirst. Nita could only stagger a few more steps, and sank down on the grass, but got up again presently, and managed to reach the tree.

When they had rested in the grateful shade of the oak for about an hour, they began the ascent, lured by the thought of the water they so needed and craved. The ravine was so long, and edged by such pathetically burnt, blighted foliage that one would not have thought there was a drop of water within fifty miles of it. But convinced that he was right, Juan struggled on up the steep ascent, and pushed his way through the brush, encouraging Nita all the while, and helping her when her courage failed or her strength gave out, which happened again and again; for the heat was intolerable, and her poor little feet were bleeding, her throat parched, her lips swollen, her whole frame one great ache.

When they had been toiling along in this way for some hours, the ravine made a sudden turn to the left, a refreshing breeze struck them, there was a little stretch of shade before them, and the brother and sister sat down to rest. They were too exhausted to talk, and in the stillness they presently heard a sound sweeter than any that could be made by Thomas's entire orchestra — the faint, silvery tinkle of falling water! Amigo heard it, too, and bounded off, and after a time came back dripping, and evidently delighted. The children had given a cry of joy, but could not move just yet. As soon as they had recovered a little they pushed on again; and, though they had some hard climbing that tired them sorely, the delicious, rippling, gushing music that got louder every moment so animated them that they grew almost brisk, and marched on until they were brought up suddenly by a cliff of rock. To go on or to go back seemed alike impossible. The cliff was not a precipice, however, and without a word Juan ran along its base until he found a tree whose top branches were nearly on a level with the ground above.

By means of this ingenious natural staircase he and Juanita mounted safely into the upper regions, and, much elated by their success, and by the pleasure of finding themselves standing on a high plateau commanding a beautiful view, getting the full benefit of the breeze, they stood looking about them with great delight for a moment, and were just about to go on in the direction from which the alluring sound came, when a bark from Amigo, followed by several whines, made them aware that they had forgotten that faithful companion with the easy ingratitude of man toward one of his truest friends. Here was a difficulty. It was clear that Amigo could not climb a tree. Suddenly Juan remembered that he had already found a way of his own to the spring, and looking over the cliff he whistled and called to him. Amigo frisked off, by way of reply, through the bushes. 'He will find us. Let us get on,' said Juan; nor had they gone far before Amigo came racing toward them, his coat covered with dust, his whole air that of Master Jack Horner when he put in his thumb and pulled out a plum — 'Oh, what a bright dog am I!' And only a little further the noise got so loud and clear that the children set

off in a sort of limping run that brought them to
the loveliest spot that had ever met their eyes, or
what seemed so at the time. It was a second,
lower cliff of gray stone to which the winds and
storms of thousands of years had given an exquisite bloom, an infinite variety of soft, neutral
tints, with here and there patches of color,
orange, red, purple, green, so wonderfully mixed
on nature's palette that an artist would have delighted to study them for weeks, and despaired of
reproducing them.

From under a ledge issued 'a thing of life' —
a beautiful little stream of the clearest, coldest
water, that danced away from under the overhanging canopy of fine old walnut, pecan, and
pollard willows, sparkled in the sunshine like
the jewel it was, and fell over the edge of the
plateau beyond. About it was a green circle of
mosses and aquatic plants, starred with water-
lilies, and fringed with quantities of maidenhair
fern. The children dimly felt the charm of the
place, but did not stop long to admire it; for a
love of nature is conspicuously absent from the
children of nature. The Indians had not taught
them to look for anything except fish in running
brooks, and they had no idea of sermons in

stones, only of the bait to be got by turning them over. But they revelled in the coolness and shade, bathed luxuriously in the water, drank as freely of it as they dared after such a long fast.

Juan had to pull Nita bodily away from the spring, and insist on her taking only a mouthful at a time. They both bathed their feet, and gradually quenched their thirst; they ate their dinner, and had a good long rest, stretched out at full length in the shade. 'This is such a nice place and I am so tired, and so are you, Juan. Casteel will never find us now. Let us stay here for several days,' said Nita. But Juan shook his head, and, getting up, reconnoitred the neighborhood in true Indian style. He was gone some little time, and Nita was beginning to feel anxious, when she saw him coming back with something in each hand, she could not tell what at that distance.

'Look here! Here is a piece of good fortune!' he called out, waving his treasure-trove in the air — a pair of old boots and a battered tin canteen. He was in high spirits. 'We need not suffer again as we have done to-day,' he said; 'these have doubtless been left by some scouting party of Texicanos. And, Nita, I am going to make you a pair of stout moccasins out of the tops of these boots so your poor feet won't be cut by the stones when we start off again.'

'Oh, don't talk of travelling any more to-day, Juan! I can't. A bird can't fly with a broken wing,' expostulated Nita. 'I can't stir. You are very good to think of making *zapatos* for me, brother mine. Can't you make a pair for yourself?'

'You will see,' replied Juan, and with his knife he soon improvised shoes for both, made Nita pick the thorns out of her feet, cut strips of leather, and bound them on for sandals, filled the canteen, and announced that he was ready to go. 'This is a well-known watering-place evidently. I find that white men have been here, and Indians. I find deer-runs leading to it, plenty of turkey-tracks, deer-tracks, some bear-tracks, a few buffalo-tracks. We will not go very far; but it won't do to stay here. Do you see those blue peaks over there? I am going there, and when I get there I shall change my course to southwest again, and shall soon snap my fingers at Casteel and every Comanche in the tribe. I know they are working on a wrong scent to-day, and now that I am this far ahead of them, I ought to be able to keep so.'

They both took another drink before leaving, and Nita gave a lingering look at the merry little mountain stream and the dense shade, as she hobbled off obediently behind Juan. Amigo, even more unwilling to leave such a pleasant spot, stood looking after them, whining piteously. He returned to his allegiance, however, at the sound of his name coaxingly pronounced by Juanita, and, where he could not understand, trusted, as became an honest and loyal dog.

Night found them plodding along through the brush, single file, in a deer-run, and before the light quite faded, Juan built a sort of bower of branches in a protected spot where there were some large rocks that also afforded partial shelter, forming as they did an angle that had only to be roofed to make a very respectable sentry-box. Into this the brother and sister crept, while Amigo mounted guard outside. They were not accustomed to being in the woods alone at any time, and Nita thought the hooting of the owls a sinister sound, the perpetual plaint of the whip-poor-will very melancholy, the whole situation most alarming. She lay awake for some time, expecting she did not know what, but something dreadful.

With Amigo outside, and his bow and arrows at his side, Juan felt none of her nervous terrors, talked and jested as if his bower were an impregnable fortress, took some food, made Nita do the same, and after throwing some small scraps to Amigo, and promising to knock over a rabbit for him next day, stretched himself out comfortably on the ground, and slept the sleep of a very tired and perfectly healthy boy. Neither he nor Nita felt the want of soft beds or downy pillows. They were quite used to doing without such luxuries, and were far less restless than the princess, in a certain fairy-story, who slept on forty feather beds.

As for their appetites next morning, they were so good they could almost have breakfasted on ten-penny nails. But alas and alack! there was nothing left in the wallet except a little corn that had been parched in the ashes. Even Amigo only took this under protest, and sniffed at it in a most ill-bred way. They were afraid to drink much from the canteen which they had filled, uncertain as they were when they should find water, and knowing that they might have

to depend for their very existence on the precious
fluid it contained. One small mouthful each
they allowed themselves before beginning the
day's journey, which lay for the most part, after
they descended the mountain, across an open
stretch of shadeless prairie. As on the previous
day, the heat was intense, the glare almost
blinding, breeze there was none, the very earth
seemed ready to blister under the fierce heat that
rayed down from the sun, and but for the shoes
that Juan had manufactured the children could
scarcely have borne that walk. Amigo called a
halt whenever they passed a tree of any kind,
and lingered in the shade as long as he could.

As the day wore on, he quite gave out; his
tongue lolled out of his mouth in a most distressing way, his eyes got a glassy look, and were
full of tears. Pitying his condition, and too kind-
hearted to see him suffer, while they had it in
their power to relieve him, Juan and Nita agreed
to stop under the first tree they came to for an
hour, and consulted as to how they should contrive to give him a drink. It was a problem, for
there were no leaves at hand out of which to
fashion a cup — none large enough, at least —
and the thirsty earth would have absorbed a sea

of water and cried out for more; but at last Juan made Nita hold up his head, while he shook from the canteen a little water at a time down the parched throat. This was a novel way for a dog to take his bitters; and, tired as the children were, they made a great frolic of it. Amigo gave them an intensely grateful look, and, after a rest, was able to go on, greatly to their relief.

Once only did they permit themselves the luxury of a sip; but, happening to turn and catch the wistful expression of Amigo's face, which said, as plainly as words could have done, 'Can't you spare me a drink from that canteen — just one?' — they stopped several times in the course of the next two hours, and relieved his throat. It was very unselfish in them, for they greatly coveted every drop; but they were doubly repaid, first by his gratitude in the very evident benefit he derived from it, and then by an occurrence of which I shall speak presently.

Even that trying, almost unbearable day, in which they felt the force of the Arabian axiom, likening great heat to the wrath of God, came to an end at last, although Nita, almost fainting under the fiery trial, thought it as interminable as it was cruel, and poor Juan, burdened with his

bow and blanket, felt ready to drop by the way-
side more than once. How thankful they were
when the shadows began to lengthen, and they
saw that the sun had almost run its course!
Before it set, Juan (who seemed to have eyes
set all around his head like a fly) caught sight
of a faint, cloud-like pillar, very distant, and
so indistinct that it was some moments before
Nita could make it out.

'There, there! off to the right! Don't you see
it?' said Juan, eagerly. 'It is the Comanches! I
knew they would think I had gone that way.'

The smoke of that camp-fire lifted a great
dread from the minds of both, and, with the
effusiveness of their race, they fell into each
other's arms, and embraced and kissed each other,
while tears of joy streamed down their cheeks.
'Ah!' said Juan, as he drew a long, free breath,
and continued to gaze at the smoky monument
of his deliverance from the house of bondage, 'I
have given you the dodge! Catch me now, if
you can, Casteel.' His eyes sparkled as he
spoke, and he walked as though his day's march
had just begun. As for Nita, her face more
than reflected his happiness, and, tired as she
was, she actually danced for joy.

'*Adios*, Casteel! *Adios todos!*' she cried out, waving her little, brown hand toward the camp, and then, with a note of regret in her voice, she added, '*Adios*, Shaneco! Shaneco was kind to us, Juan. I shall never forget that.'

'We shall never see them any more,' said Juan. 'We can walk where we please now, on hard ground or soft, in sand or mud. And we can take our own time, and need not travel in the middle of the day. And do you say now that we shall never see our mother, Nita? *Viva! Viva! Viva!*'

Nita joined in this shout, and Amigo, not understanding the demonstration, barked once or twice interrogatively; then, seeing from the children's faces that the excitement was a joyous one, tried feebly to frisk, whereupon both of the children embraced him, told him that he would soon be back at the *hacienda*, assured him that he should live upon *pan de gloria* and cream for the rest of his natural life, and declared that he was the dearest dog in the world, the most intelligent, the most affectionate, and the handsomest. When Amigo had duly responded to these speeches, Juan remembered that he had seen a creek just before the great discovery, and had meant to explore it.

'It looks very dry,' he said, when they reached it; 'but it is running in the direction of our route, and we may have the luck to find some water. I should give a buffalo-robe for a good drink if I had it. I am almost choked, Nita.'

He spoke cheerfully, but had little expectation of coming upon a pool, and what he had, dwindled as he went on and saw that the shallow stream had as completely disappeared as though it had never existed. All at once, when Juan had grown very serious under the gravity of the responsibility he had assumed, and was thinking with dismay of the empty canteen and wallet, Amigo bounded past him and began trotting along with his nose close to the ground, sniffing excitedly here and there.

'What is he after?' asked Nita; but before Juan could reply Amigo had stopped near some big rocks, and had begun scratching in the sand with all his might and main.

'Water!' shouted Juan, and he was right; for when he and Nita fell on their knees and began scooping out the sand from the hole Amigo had made, they found in a little while that it was no longer dry sand, but wet — a fact that put so much energy into their excavations that they soon got down to fresh water. Amigo's instinct had divined the hidden spring, and had saved them, as they had saved him, much suffering. It was almost joy enough to watch it as it welled up from its beneficent source, so pure, cold, clear — so beautiful and sweetly satisfying in that arid waste. It seemed as though the children would never be done dabbling in it, drinking of it, pouring it out lavishly about them. Amigo was drenched with it more than once, and appeared to revel in the experience.

Hunger was far more endurable now that thirst no longer tormented them; and, infinitely refreshed, if wofully hungry, they betook themselves to bed — not a bed of roses, but one of dried grasses, having above a majestic canopy 'with God's name writ on it in worlds.' How their mother's heart would have yearned over them if she could have seen those two little figures lying out there under the stars in tranquil sleep; so young, so helpless, completely at the mercy of the world, environed by a thousand dangers; yet perfectly safe — as safe in that lonely wilderness as in the most populous city protected by omnipresent love, shielded, perhaps, by a devoted mother's prayers, and watched over by guardian angels such as we are told 'do always behold the face of our Father'!

Whether it was that Amigo did not arouse them, or that the fear of the Comanches no longer troubled their dreams, the sun was quite high before either Juan or Nita stirred. Their breakfast was not a very elaborate one, consisting as it did of a drink of water apiece, and they were only detained until the canteen could be filled.

'We shall get to the peak before sunset,' said Juan, 'and I am sure there is plenty of game in the hills, and I will kill enough to last us for some days; so cheer up, *hermanita mia*. We are not going to starve while I have got Shaneco's bow and so much as a single arrow left.'

'I am not so very hungry, Juan. I shall do very well to-day. I had more than you did from the wallet, and feel quite strong,' said Nita brightly. 'I don't mind anything now that Casteel is not behind us.'

'Oh, that is all right! They will not follow us any farther, but will go home,' replied Juan, and this was what happened.

The Indians probably thought that their rebellious captives would certainly die in the wilderness, either by violence or from starvation, and, content with this vengeance, gave up the chase and returned to their encampment on the clear fork of the Brazos. If they had not been under treaty just then with the United States, they might have made the search for Juan and Nita a side issue of one of their raids, and, in that event, would almost certainly have recaptured them; but, as it was, it did not seem to them worth while to go to any more trouble to catch and kill two children who were sure to perish if left to themselves.

There was a kind of rivalry between the brother and sister all that morning as to which should seem to have least felt the fatigue and deprivations of the last few days. It was well for both that they had learned fortitude in a severe school, or they would certainly have broken down under an exact repetition of the previous day's experience. They never could have borne it if they had been accustomed to a life of luxury and indulgence and been tenderly nurtured. As is was, Romulus and Remus were not more roughly reared. The only experience they had had of a woman's care since their capture was when Shaneco's wife and the other squaws had

taken them out (together with the other children
of the tribe) and put them through a half-
medical, half-disciplinary course of torture which
consisted in harrowing up their young flesh with
a row of long thorns inserted in a piece of wood.
The child that cried or failed to bear its pain
in perfect silence, the child that begged to be
spared, or tried to escape, was always soundly
beaten, and held up to public contempt beside
as lacking in courage and endurance.

One piece of Comanche discipline consisted in
making the older children do without sleep or
food for as long as their instructors thought
necessary, and still another in making them perform arduous tasks, and run or walk great
distances while deprived of their natural rest,
or fasting. The warriors of the future were, of
course, subjected to more severe tests than the
girls, whose lives were to be more inglorious and
homely, but all were in some measure subjected
to these agreeable educational influences. An
Indian lad gloried in his capacity for suffering,
and scorned himself if, at the close of three
nights of wakefulness, he fell asleep between the
admonishing cuts that he received from the
squaw in charge — a grim old figure with a

bundle of rods in her hand, and determination in her eye.

So now, although our poor babes in the woods were footsore and weary and hungry, they made no complaint, but trudged on hour after hour under the burning sun with great patience and courage, stopping when they could go no farther, and taking such refreshment as the sickeningly warm water in the canteen afforded. By noon they had made their way to a small thicket of mesquite about five miles from the peak. This offered a mitigation of the distressing glare of the plain, rather than anything that could be called shade; and here the children dropped down on the hot earth without strength enough to have carried them another yard, every vital force being completely drained out of them for the time.

The confidence with which Juan had started out had vanished like the morning dew under that terrible sun. It seemed to him that they had lain down to die. How was he to know that there was game in the hills? How were they even to get there? What were they to do for water, now that the canteen was again empty? Too proud to express his dejection, and not understanding in the least that it arose from physical causes, he turned his back on Nita, and threw his arm up over his head, and lay perfectly motionless for so long that Nita got seriously uneasy. When she could stand this strange conduct no longer, she pulled anxiously at his sleeve, saying, 'Juan! Juan! What is the matter with you? Are you ill? Look here! Answer me!'

But Juan would not answer and still hid his face. He did not know that he was distressing Nita, and wanted to be as miserable as he pleased. Presently a wail of despair reached him, and, turning over, he saw Nita who was weeping piteously, overcome by visions of Juan dying and dead, leaving her alone in the wilderness. *'Oh, oh, mi madre, mi madre! Quiero mi madre!'* sobbed the unhappy child. Her love for Juan and her admiration of him were unbounded; she had perfect faith in his ability to do anything and everything; but when that support failed her, she collapsed altogether, so accustomed was she to lean her whole weight on him. Juan was evidently hopeless or very ill, and in either event she was miserable.

The sight of his dear little sister's wretchedness appealed so strongly to Juan's manly and generous nature that he sat up at once, and affected a good deal more liveliness than he felt. *'Pobrecita! Pobrecita!* what is it? Don't cry. You will see our mother soon. What afflicts you?' he demanded, soothingly.

Nita now opened her heart, and Juan, ashamed of having ever seemed to desert so dependent a creature, tried to talk her and himself back into renewed hope.

'It isn't that I am hungry. Don't worry about that, Juan. But you must be ravenous,' said Nita, when her tranquillity was restored.

Juan would not confess this; but the very mention of the subject set both to thinking of a tantalizing variety of dishes in the silence that followed. 'What makes you silent, Nita?' asked Juan, at last.

'I was thinking that I wished I had one of our mother's *tortillas* — only one. You should have it if I had; I am not hungry,' persisted Nita.

'Why, that is what I was thinking,' said Juan, 'only I wished for a whole basketful. Wouldn't you like a *peloncilla*, Nita?'

'Or a *tamale*, Juan?'

'Or a cheese, Nita?'

'Or a watermelon?' she replied; but this duet had excited Juan's imagination unduly.

'Ah! you are starved, poor child! You are thirsty and tired to death! Oh! if I only had some water and food for you!' and he threw himself down again on his back with a deep sigh. It was Nita's turn now to comfort him; but, although he got some strength from her affection, her asurances that all would yet be well did not find much of an echo.

It was now getting a little cooler, and the world was less like a vast oven. Amigo, who had been stretched out comfortably under a tree, and had stood the day's journey better than they had expected, came up to Juan and snuffed about him restlessly, doubtless with the intention of admonishing him that they ought to be off again. But Juan did not move, and had not the energy to respond to any such demand. Even when the afternoon had almost all gone, he continued to lie there, inertly, a prey to gloomy doubts and fears.

When he did get up it was with a bound that brought him to his feet at once, and of which he would not have believed himself capable a moment before. 'Look! Look!' he cried, pointing above them, and obeying, Nita saw overhead, beautifully outlined against a deep-blue sky, a large flock of snow-white doves flying toward the peak.

'It is near sundown, and they are seeking water and a place to roost. See how straight they are flying toward the hills. We will follow. I was right. It can't be very far. Come on, Nita,' said Juan, all excited interest now. 'I will help you if you can't get along by yourself.'

Led by this lovely band of birds, the children struggled bravely and hopefully on for another mile, when they were still further cheered to see a long line of fine trees about a half-mile beyond them, which they knew must be growing on the banks of a considerable stream. Amazed now at the frame of mind that had produced such a profound depression, and delighted to know that succor was so close at hand, Juan never stopped except to encourage his companions, until they had reached one of those clear, swift, charming streams in which that region abounds.

As they approached it, a deer occasionally bounded off in front of them, or a drove of turkeys went whirring aside out of their way; but, although both Juan and Juanita strung their bows, neither could get near enough for a shot. Amigo started a rabbit and gave it a tight race, but with no better result. There seemed little chance of their getting a supper, and they were blue enough about it; but when they got to the river, what should they see but quantities of fish almost praying to be caught! Scarcely stopping to bathe his face and get a drink, Juan promptly cut a willow pole, fastened his line to it, found a grasshopper, baited his hook, and let fly, while Nita, sure of the result, ran about with surprising alacrity, picking up dry wood for a fire. Nor had Juan to wait long for a bite, for such was the touching primeval innocence of the fish that no sooner did the grasshopper light on the water than there was a grand rush and scramble among them to get to it. A large, fine trout was soon flopping around on the gravelly margin of the river. Two others joined him in swift succession; and, too hungry to wait another moment, Juan dropped his pole, seized, cleaned these, cut them up, ran sticks through each morsel, and, with Nita's help, soon had them in front of the fire. It seemed to them that the fish would never be cooked; but after an eternity of waiting they were done. And oh, how brown, crisp, delicious, incomparable they were, and what a feast it was!

CHAPTER V

JUAN MAKES A DISCOVERY

WHEN the two weary starvelings had partaken as freely of their ambrosial repast of broiled fish as they dared after so long a fast, their one thought was a place in which to rest. This, Juan undertook to select, although, as he limped off into the woods, he could scarcely drag one foot after another.

If he had been alone, he could not have resisted the temptation to sink down anywhere, so painful was any further effort; but he had Nita to consider, and her comfort and safety required that he should reconnoitre the immediate neighborhood and choose some sheltered spot for the night's resting-place. Leaden weights seemed to have attached themselves to his usually nimble feet; and he could not have felt more bruised if he had been pounded in a mortar for the last two days. But he persevered, and in about half an hour came back to Nita, walking, indeed, as slowly as though he had been his own grandfather, but with a bright face that promised pleasant news.

'Come, little sister!' he said affectionately, holding out his hand to help her to her feet.

'Oh, Juan, indeed, indeed, I can't move an inch! Don't ask me to get up!' remonstrated Nita plaintively.

But Juan, with a smile, insisted, telling her that he had something nice to show her. Then he put his arm around her and carried her off, whistling to Amigo, who, with his head on one side, was making dreadful faces over his fish-bones, and positively declined to follow anybody just then.

Nita had not far to go. At the end of five minutes' walk, Juan stopped, his progress impeded apparently by a large rock. The river rippled away in a long, shining curve on his right, and on the left rose a high bluff.

'This way!' he said, and in a flash he had disappeared completely.

'Why, where have you gone? Where are you, Juan?' cried Nita, when she had skirted the rock and could see nothing of her brother.

She was answered by a merry shout with a queer ring in it:

'Here! here! Don't you see me?'

It sounded very near, and she stared all about

her, up the bluff, into the trees, into the river
even; and then, taking a good look at the rock,
she saw Juan's laughing face peeping at her from
behind the leaves of a bush that grew in the
angle formed by the bluff and the rock.

'Come here! You can just squeeze in, when you
push the bush aside,' said Juan encouragingly;
and the next moment Nita was standing in delighted astonishment inside a beautiful little cave.

'I discovered it quite by accident,' explained
Juan. 'I saw a rabbit dart in here and looked
to see where he had gone. It is perfectly dry and
warm, and there are no snake-holes, for I have
looked all about it for them; and here we can
stay just as long as we please. We are as safe as
though we were at home. Aren't you glad you
came, now? Isn't it a splendid thing to have a
house of our own?' He threw himself down with
a sigh of deep content as he spoke.

And Nita, who had thought she could not take
another step, explored every corner of the cave
again and again, and indulged in the most rap-
turous comments on it. '*O! La buena fortuna!
Qué casa segura, bonisima, hermosa, grandisima!*'
('Oh, what good fortune! What a safe, nice, fine,
big house!') she cried, and was not half done ad-

miring it then. The last sounds Juan heard that
night were, 'Oh, isn't it just too delightful, too
fortunate for anything!' from Nita, and a loud
snore from Amigo, who had traced them without
the least difficulty, and had promptly sought
the repose he needed, and after a day spent in
the open air and violent exercise enjoyed such
profound and refreshing slumber as rarely falls
to the lot of dwellers in cities.

Happy and secure, they all slept on, and on,
until even the cave was quite bright. When at
last they did awake, it was to find themselves the
stiffest, lamest creatures in the world, and the
day well advanced. It seemed at first as if every
motion of the body would result in the dislocation
of a joint. But when people have to find, as well
as to cook their own breakfasts, they cannot lie
abed; so, with many an exclamation and groan,
Nita took herself off to the river to perform her
morning ablutions; and Juan, after making some
wry faces and yawning prodigiously, followed
her example.

The fresh air soon put new life into them,
while exercise became first endurable and then
enjoyable. Nita built a fire in Comanche fashion.
Juan got out his fishing-pole, and gave himself

JUAN GOT OUT HIS FISHING-POLE, AND GAVE HIMSELF UP TO THE
BUSINESS OF THE MOMENT

up to the business of the moment. The lesson
of the previous evening, however, had not been
wasted on those Arcadian trout. They had lost
confidence in man and grasshoppers, and they
now kept back a little, prudently waiting to see
whether further experience would destroy or
confirm their suspicions. It was a blundering,
stupid catfish, after all, that darted at the bait,
swallowed it, made a desperate plunge below —
and snapped Juan's line!

'My only hook!' exclaimed Juan, quite aghast,
as he saw the cord disappear, and drew in what
remained of it.

'Good Heavens! What shall we do?' lamented
Nita, who, like Juan, was looking forward to her
breakfast, now that she might indulge her appetite without danger. They had mutually confided to each other only a moment before that
they were 'as hungry as wolves,' and visions of
trout browned to a turn had haunted them ever
since they had opened their eyes. But if there's
many a slip between the cup and the lip, there
are more between fish and the frying-pan, or any
substitute for one; and for a few minutes it
seemed as though the children were destined to
be defeated by the fishes.

But Juan was by no means at the end of his resources, and he presently went poking about and around in a purposeful sort of way, saying: 'I know what I'll do! Just wait a minute.'

And this is what he did: He found a small bone, not much larger than a quill, and, having sharpened one end, he tied his line to the bone within an inch of the sharp end, leaving three or four inches beyond. He then tied the gills of a fish to the long and blunt end of the bone. Then he took a piece of dry wood about five feet long, and, having fastened his line to it, threw the wood out into the deep water. The next minute he saw the wood give a dash and begin travelling off at odd angles, taking an occasional dive under the water, and popping up again where least expected. Into the clear water jumped Juan, creating a great excitement among its innocent inhabitants. The wood now rushed upstream at an amazing pace, Juan swimming after it with long and dexterous side-strokes, while Nita, on the bank, shrieked with laughter as she watched the queer race. It was a triumphant moment when Juan got hold of the wood and towed his prize to the shore. It proved to be an immense flat-headed catfish, weighing thirty or forty pounds, and great was the young fisher's pride and joy.

It was a troublesome piece of business for Juan to get his patent hook out of the fish's throat, until he hit on the masterly plan of cutting off its head; this so simplified matters that he soon had his tackle clear. The fact that their breakfast had so nearly escaped them gave it added zest, though this was scarcely needed. A more hearty and entirely satisfactory meal was never made, and Amigo got two large pieces without any bones for his share.

The afternoon was given up to lounging and talking. The children reviewed all their past life at home and among the Comanches, and it was agreed that they should stay in their present comfortable quarters until they had entirely recovered, and had laid by such provisions as they could carry. In this way the risk of starvation would be considerably lessened. On this subject Nita had an inspiration.

'I can carry a good deal, and you can take some, and why shouldn't Amigo help us?' she exclaimed. 'If there are pack-horses, why shouldn't there be pack-dogs?'

Such an idea had never occurred to Juan; but

he highly approved of it now. While they were still discussing the subject, they heard the gobble of approaching turkeys. The evening was drawing down, and the birds were coming in, as usual, to roost near the river.

'We are not going to live on fish altogether,' said Juan, and straightway began to imitate the notes of the turkeys with the aid of a little box cut out of cedar-wood. Shaneco had taught him this important piece of wood-craft, and had shown him how to make this 'yelper,' or turkey-call, and how to produce the proper tones, by scraping away on one side with a bit of slate.

And I will tell you how it was done, in case any of you should be captured by Comanches and make your escape, or drift out into the great West, or summer in the Adirondacks, or somewhere at some time wish to lure wild turkeys into your power. There are several kinds of these sinfully deceptive contrivances; but the very best and most effective, according to a Texan Leather-stocking of my acquaintance, is made in this way: Take of any soft wood — poplar is best — a piece four inches long, one inch wide, and two deep. With a three-quarter auger, bore holes one and three quarters inches deep, near enough together to allow you to cut out with your pocket-knife between them a cavity in the block of wood three inches long, two and one half deep and three quarters wide. The wood on one side of the box should be one eighth inch thick — the side held toward you in using it. The side used to imitate the turkeys should be worked down quite thin with a sharp knife, and sand-papered; indeed, the sound is improved when the whole box is made very smooth. So far most 'yelpers' agree; but my acquaintance claims to have discovered by accident an important thing greatly affecting the tone. He says that if (when your box is complete) you will take your knife and in the thin side of it split a cut two and one half inches long, you will find that it gives to perfection the peculiar 'kyonk' of a wild turkey. It is in effect very like dropping a key or other foreign object on the keys of a piano, and gives the same curious twanging note. So perfect is the imitation, he tells me, he has often hidden in the weeds and called turkeys up near enough to have knocked them over with the muzzle of his gun, had he chosen to do anything so unsportsmanlike.

But, to go back, Juan and Nita both were ambitious of getting a shot at the turkeys, so they strung their bows and hid in some bushes near a large oak, in which they fancied the fowls would roost. Juan laid a few arrows down beside him, in case the first shot was a failure, though he thought this an unlikely event.

'Oh, do you think you will hit one? I do hope you won't miss!' whispered Nita, excitedly, as the unsuspicious fowls marched down to the river to drink before settling down, or rather up, for the night.

'Hit one?' repeated Juan scornfully; 'I should rather think I would.'

He then fell to scraping on his 'yelper' again, and presently the whole flock came hopping and skipping and gobbling toward the children, and almost ran over them! Embarrassed by this wealth of opportunity, they aimed first at one and then at another, until it seemed as if the whole flock would pass without either of the young hunters getting a shot. Juan finally selected his bird, and shot, but missed. Last in the procession came a sober, staid old gobbler, which stopped a moment within ten feet of Nita. Whiz! went her arrow square into its breast. As he turned to run off, the head of the arrow struck the ground, which pushed the sharp iron point

right through him, spitting him as it were as if
in preparation for roasting; so, after running a few
yards with drooping wings, it tumbled over.

Up jumped Nita, so transported by her success
that she paid no attention to Juan's warning
'*Cuidado!*' ('Look out!') and seized the turkey
by the neck.

'You will get hurt!' shouted Juan, running up;
but the turkey had already made such lively
play with its wings and feet that she had released
it. 'Well, well, Nita, I am proud of you!' he said,
a little condescendingly. 'But something must
be the matter with my bow. I believe I could
have done better with the old one.' He carefully
examined his bow as he spoke, but found it all
right. 'It wasn't my fault, I know!' he protested
with some pique.

'Perhaps the turkeys were at fault,' suggested
Nita teasingly.

'Nonsense! How ridiculous you are to talk so!
Do you mean to say that I don't know how to
shoot?' demanded Juan rather angrily; and without waiting for her reply he walked off to look
up his arrow. He found it, and came back with
it, saying, triumphantly, 'I knew it! It was the
arrow. See here, how it is warped! It was all the

fault of this crooked thing. I must be more careful in future, and do as Shaneco told me. "Always straighten your arrows before you start
out to hunt or fight," he said. I remember now;
but it was so long ago I had forgotten.'

With this he picked up the turkey, and walked
back to camp in dignified silence. It was cooked
for their supper in the open air; and then Nita,
who liked the idea of playing at housekeeping,
built a small fire of very dry wood near the mouth
of the cave.

This served to light the farthest corner of their
apartment, making it indeed a cheerful retreat
for the merry little party that assembled in the
cave, when darkness dropped suddenly down, as
the darkness always does in that land of brief
twilights. There was fish, warmed over, and the
breast of that delicious turkey, which was greatly
relished; there was much laughter and chatter;
Amigo was caressed and complimented, and fed
with now a wing, now a leg, until his eyes
glistened with satisfaction.

For such a gentlemanly dog, his table-manners
were not good; and he had the arrears of several
days to make up — days of unaccustomed deprivation followed by a fish-diet not at all to his

taste; so when, after all his mute pantomime,
which it seemed to him that even a man would
understand, Juan cut short his repast with a very
small, undesirable bone and a curt 'Be off, sir!
Go and lie down,' Amigo rebelled, and snatched
at the coveted carcass before him. Juan would
have beaten him *à la* Shaneco, I am afraid, but
Nita threw her arms around the culprit's neck,
and begged him off, after which Amigo slunk
guiltily away to a corner of the cave, and peace
was restored.

So secure and at ease were the children that
by a natural process of association they began to
talk of certain gala-days that they remembered
at the *hacienda;* this led to the old, ever new,
subject — their mother; and the evening closed
with '*Mañanitas Allegras,*' [1] '*El Sueño,*' [2] and one
or two more of the old songs.

'We must push on as soon as we get some food.
Our mother has waited so long for us, we must
not linger,' said Juan, in final comment; and,
much as Nita dreaded the hardships and dangers
that awaited them, she assented to this, though
rather quaveringly, as she looked about her and
thought of the world beyond that safe retreat.

[1] 'Happy mornings.'   [2] 'The dream.'

'No, we must not stay. We must go to her.
It may not be so bad. And if it is, we must suffer,
since our mother is waiting. Poor, sweet, little
mother! Ah, if we were only birds, and could
fly to you!' she said.

'And be shot, perhaps, on the wing,' said Juan.
'As for me, I prefer to walk.'

The children were up at daylight next morning,
being now thoroughly rested and restored to
their usual state of perfect health and gleeful
spirits. The squirrels darting about in the trees
outside were not more full of joyous life; and
even Amigo was all bounds, and frisks, and
cheerfulness, as different as possible from the
dog that crossed the prairie with drooping head
and tail, bowed down by the weight of his woes.
After breakfast the trio went on an exploring expedition about their camp, having been too tired
on the previous day to do anything except provide for their immediate necessities. Not a very
sober ramble did it prove, for the way in which
they swarmed up trees and jumped from one to
another, slid down the bank, dived into the river,
floated, swam, and played there until they were
tired, scrambled out again, chased one another
over the prairie, pulled a harmless snake out of

its hole, diffused themselves generally over the neighborhood in search of amusement and adventure, would have frightened elderly persons of civilized habits quite out of their wits (if any such had been there to witness the children's antics), and would have turned a mother, a governess, or a nurse gray in less than an hour by the clock. As it was, they took their fill of frolic without fear and without reproach or interference.

The rabbits scudded away from them, were pursued, ran up the white flag, and for the most part escaped, though one was knocked over by Juan in the course of the morning. The hawks overhead turned a curious eye upon them; but finding out that they were not a new and interesting variety of poultry, lost interest in them, and sailed indifferently away. The smaller birds flew up before them out of the tall grass, disclosing nests in which were eggs that never developed into the third brood of the season, for they were promptly sucked by Juan and Juanita, who were connoisseurs in the matter of nature's edibles. Neither guardian, mentor, teacher, pastor, nor master these children had; they were as free as air; but, after all, they did not greatly abuse their liberty. They tired of play about noon, and bethought themselves of dinner. At least Nita did. Juan had feasted on berries, and was not yet ready to go back to camp.

'I think I see some vines over there,' he said to Nita, who was resting from her pleasures. 'I'll be back presently, and will bring you enough berries for dinner and supper. Wait here for me.' He darted off as he spoke, and in about ten minutes Nita was surprised to hear a shout of joy from him. 'Come here, Nita! Just look here!' he called out; and she rushed after him, all curiosity to know what this demonstration meant.

She found him gazing with delight at a mass of nicely sealed honeycomb neatly packed away under a ledge of rock. There it was, in full view; and how tempting it was! But, alas! it was much above their reach. Now, if there was one thing that the children liked, it was honey. It took the place of all the candy, bonbons, cakes, custards, méringues, and jams in which other children delight; and to see it and not to be able to get at it was simply distracting.

Both Juan and Nita danced about on the grass below in their impatience, and looked, and longed and looked again, without being able to think of a way to rifle the sweets. They ran up and down, gave their views as to the way it was to be done, tried to jump up, and to crawl up, although there was scarcely footing for a fly on the face of the rock, almost quarrelled as to methods, and at last relapsed into silence only to stare anew at the treasure so cunningly placed where, as Nita said, 'no one could get it.'

'I don't know about that,' said Juan; and, running into the bed of the creek, he picked up a young tree, long dead, and washed down by some flood. This he propped up against the rock to serve him as a ladder. He then looked about until he found a dagger-plant (*Yucca filamentosa*), and armed with one of its sharp leaves he climbed up near the ledge, Nita looking on, the while, with the most intense interest. He thrust the dagger into the comb, and a generous flood of clear, golden syrup bedewed it and trickled down the face of the rock, like rich tears, which Juan would have liked to catch and bottle, Egyptian fashion.

But out, also, rushed a swarm of angry bees and fairly enveloped him, making so savage a sortie, and putting so much sting into their buzz, and so much buzz into their sting, that even Juan, the daring, was only too glad to scramble, almost tumble, down again. He brushed off such bees as still clung to him, and made light of his wounds, but he did not offer to repeat the experiment.

He and Nita were now more piqued and aggravated than ever; for, after tasting the delicious honey that still clung to the dagger-leaf, it seemed an insupportable deprivation to get no more. So, after scraping off the last drop, and rolling his eyes at Nita in sympathetic enjoyment, Juan determined that he would not be beaten by any colony of bees that ever swarmed, buzzed, or stung. Off he started again, and this time brought back a long, light pole, on the end of which he tied his butcher's knife. He then made Nita sweep away all leaves and dust from the flat stones at the bottom of the cliff, and cover it with large fresh leaves. This done, he advanced again on the enemy, going very cautiously up the ladder this time. While still at a safe distance, he managed to cut off a large piece of comb, which rolled below and was at once picked up by Nita, while a golden cascade poured over the ledge and dropped into the vessel prepared to catch it. Astonished to find the bees quiet, Juan mounted higher and higher. He now saw that his enemies were completely demoralized, as many a better army has been by the richness of spoils.

No sooner was the comb broken by his first dagger-thrust, than every bee bade instant farewell to industry, prudence, foresight, valor, and every other virtue for which that insect is noted, and, falling upon the abundant supply of honey disclosed, it seized and carried off all it could lay feelers on. It never so much as occurred to the bees to sting anybody, so absorbed were they in plundering the cells that they had built and filled with nectar.

When Juan saw this, he unbound his knife; he threw away the pole, and, leaning forward, cut the remainder of the comb loose; and it bounded down below, burying untold bees deep in its recesses. Those which could leave it did so, and settled back on their hive; but when Nita, who had run away in a fright, came back, it took her some time to remove the dead and wounded. Juan came down with a beaming air of victory, and, taking up as much honey as they could carry, the children walked back to the cave, well satisfied with their ramble and its results.

Fresh fish, wild turkey, dewy berries, and rich honey made a dinner which an epicure would not have despised, and with which Juan and Nita certainly found no fault. It was served under a wide-spreading oak, from an extremely æsthetic green dinner-service of broad, cool leaves, beautiful in color and texture. It was washed down with '*agua pura, limpia, deliciosa*,' [1] according to Juan, who brought the sparkling liquid from the river in other leaves pinned together with thorns, so as to form goblets. And I am afraid the Señora would have been alarmed if she had seen the way in which the viands disappeared before her two healthy, hungry children.

When dinner was over, they bethought themselves of the remainder of the honey, and went back to get it and store it. As they approached the spot they were surprised to see it through a cloud of bees, as it were; and they soon discovered that a grand battle, a regular Waterloo of a struggle, was going on between two armies of bees — the owners of the hive and some neighboring and thievish soldiers of fortune that had been attracted by the smell of the honey.

[1] Pure, clear, delicious water.

After a really terrible conflict, the home bees, animated, no doubt, by a deep sentiment of devotion to their hearths and honeysides, drove off the wicked marauders.

But they were not destined to occupy that 'sweet, sweet home' again; for, no sooner was their victory complete than Juan reaped its fruits. Casting about for some means of carrying the honey, after some reflection he got a couple of willow poles; across these he laid large pieces of bark which he tore from the trees; and, having thus constructed a sort of litter, he laid the honeycomb on it, and, with himself at one end and Nita at the other, the golden treasure was borne to the cave. The young bearers had to move very steadily, and to pick their way carefully, but they only dropped one piece of the comb on the road, and that they recovered.

They had to leave a good deal behind them in its fluid form, and Nita proposed to fill the canteen with it, but Juan insisted that that must be kept for water alone, and asked her rather sarcastically whether if she were out on the prairie in a burning sun again, she would enjoy quenching her thirst with honey. Nita readily gave up the point, and Juan then said that he would make something for the purpose. He announced this confidentially, as though there had been a tin-shop at the next turning, and he master of the art of making pots and pans. 'I can't do it just now; but you just wait a bit,' he said, with the air of a person who is too modest to say so, but believes that he can do anything. It cannot be denied that Juan was somewhat vain of his exceptional strength, intelligence, and boldness. It had given him a good deal of prominence even among the Comanches, and it was natural that he should accept the popular estimate of himself, especially as Nita unconsciously encouraged it by believing in him even more implicitly than he did in himself, and there was no one at hand to point out his fault and teach him to correct it.

It was a fortunate thing, under the circumstances, that he had such unbounded self-reliance; it stood him in good stead in the course of that journey of perils, vicissitudes, uncertainties. Timidity and distrustfulness would have been fatal qualities then and there.

That evening Juan left his sister to her own devices, and, taking his bow and 'yelper' went on a private and particular hunting expedition of his own, from which he returned with two

large gobblers and a turkey-hen of the plumpest
and most satisfactory proportions.

They spent the next day in getting a good supply of cooked provisions, and that night was their
last in their pretty little cave. Nita abandoned
it next morning with lively regret and a troubled
anticipation of evils to come. But far stronger
than this sense of fear was that impelling power
that can send the youngest, gentlest, most timid
creature in the world into unknown dangers, and
to death if need be — the power of love. Neither
Nita nor Juan could resist the mighty force of a
mother's love that was drawing them across three
hundred miles of wilderness, straight to the
mother-heart that generated it. And so, with a
sigh or two, Nita put her little hand in Juan's,
and walked away from the place that for the last
few days had been their haven of refuge.

Still bearing away to the southwest, Juan
crossed the river at a shallow ford about half a
mile below the cave, and struck out into the open
country beyond. They took a last look at the
pleasant stream as it rushed around a curve and
was broken into music by the obstructing stones
beyond. Juan threw a pebble at a moccasin-
snake gliding about near the bank; Amigo, who

was enjoying a last swim, came out and shook himself; and now there was no longer an excuse for lingering. The cave was again empty; the fish were again gliding about fearlessly in the cool, clear, quiet depths of the river; the children were again facing the unknown.

CHAPTER VI

MIRAGE

THE next few days passed without bringing any serious mishaps or startling adventures to the children. Knowing that they were provided with food, and were fresh, Juan made rather long marches; but there were some circumstances that made them quite tolerable, even enjoyable. On the first and second days they were so fortunate as to come upon one small stream (in process of drying up, a process happily, not yet complete) and two pools, all that remained, of similar streams. In the heat of the day they lay by and further refreshed themselves by taking a nap. They saw deer and turkeys in the distance, and several times wolves, quite near, who showed their teeth savagely when Amigo ran after them. Juan and Nita were in terror lest he should be killed, and not too sure that they would not share the same fate; but that Fabian animal always fell back on his reënforcements without risking a pitched battle, and when the children came up, the wolves always slunk off, leaving

Amigo a kind of cheap victor, admired both for his courage and prudence.

On the third day they were blessed with cloudy skies, and seemed, moreover, to have got into a little belt of country where the drought had not been so severe, or where, perhaps, it had been mitigated by light rains. It was not only delightful to see how much greener the foliage and grass looked, but the wild flowers fairly carpeted the prairie, and made of it a vast garden. Nita, who loved flowers, was enraptured by their variety and beauty, and was always begging Juan to stop and look at this or that one, quite without success. They walked for miles and miles through what seemed a sea of blue lupins, the long, wave-like undulations of the plains creating the most exquisite effects of light and shade. If Nita had chosen, she could have gathered more than thirty varieties of phlox alone; and, as it was, her hands were full of Indian pride, Sweet-William, Stars-of-Bethlehem, snap-dragon, heather-bells. There were occasional bursts of sunlight in the morning; the afternoon was gray, and threatened rain. But there was a clear sunset after all, and a gorgeous one, nor had it quite faded when they came upon a most lovely little lake guarded by three tall cottonwoods that seemed to be etched against the sky. Here they camped, and supped, and slept. Nita, her head pillowed on Amigo, saw the stars shining tenderly in the placid water, and idly tried to count them, but was in dreamland long before she had numbered so much as fifty of the 'fine patines of gold' in the floor of heaven.

On the fourth day they had a sun that seemed the fiercer for his temporary eclipse; but, by making a détour, Juan got into a fine stretch of forest, in whose cool shade they walked for miles, indeed, until high noon, when not even the finely arched, delightful canopy overhead could altogether shut out the heat and light that the sun had darted or sifted into the favored spot, a ray at a time. It was no longer cool or dark, or even green, except by comparison, for they could now see how dry the earth was, and the vegetation was pining, one might almost say panting, for the moisture it craved. But it was still sheltered; so they leaned against two trees and fanned themselves with a fan of leaves and twigs, and when they were entirely rested and had tired of shying stones at the squirrels, their neighbors, they dined, and made the usual halt, but it was not quite as long as usual.

After looking out on the broad expanse of prairie that stretched out before him, Juan got restless. He saw that it offered no shelter of any kind for a great distance; he knew that the canteen was not more than half full, and he determined to travel as far as possible that evening. Nita was hurried off, therefore, as soon as it was possible to start, and was not allowed to stop again until it was quite dark, when he gave her hour in which to rest and get her supper, and, to her surprise and dismay, insisted on travelling three hours longer by starlight. It was still starlight when he awoke her, and told her to eat sparingly, for a full meal would require full rations of water, announcing, as well, that he meant to resume his march at once.

'Why, it isn't light yet! and I am so sleepy and so tired, dear Juan. Do go to sleep again,' remonstrated Nita, not understanding what the need was for all this haste. But Juan, fortunately, was firm, and by his decision doubtless saved their lives.

'Don't eat any honey,' he also said to Nita; but this command she thought absurd and tyrannical, and helped herself to a good, big piece when his back was turned. The very last drop of water was given to Amigo before they started, the children having had their share previously.

They had made about ten miles when up came their enemy, the sun, strong and fierce and bright, ready for his day's journey, while they were already tired and thirsty. After a brief rest they went on again; but their steps and spirits flagged sadly in the next four hours, the first getting slower and the last dropping lower with every moment spent under the almost vertical rays of the relentless sun. The heat soon increased to a degree that made any exertion first painful and then impossible. At last they sank down together in the open plain, and looked about them wearily —up at the cloudless sky above them, the fissures in the earth at their feet, and the grass around them, yellowed by the long drought, with here and there the ghost of what had once been a flower shrivelling on its stalk, the peak dimly visible on the edge of the horizon, and hardly to be distinguished from the clouds.

For about an hour they sat there in silent, patient suffering, and then very gradually a merciful veil of thin clouds was drawn over the brazen heavens, and mitigated their wretchedness. It seemed possible again to live and breathe, although the air was still so sultry that they felt suffocated. It was also possible to eat something — not much, it is true, but that little revived them considerably; but already the want of water was beginning to be painfully felt, especially by the wilful Nita.

Juan's mind was oppressed by anxious fears for the morrow. Look as he would, he could see no evidence of forest or stream, and the day's experience had shown him what he had to expect, with no shelter, no water, and that sun shining perhaps full upon him from dawn until dark. The more he thought of it the more unhappy he grew, and the result showed how well-founded his apprehensions were. His solicitude for Nita added fifty-fold to his anxieties. He was quite harsh to her when she proposed to camp where they were; and as soon as it grew cooler entered upon a long and very fatiguing march, for darkness and night were now precious. He did not require that it should be rapidly made — that would have been a sheer impossibility; but it was imperatively necessary that they should traverse as much of that apparently interminable prairie lying before them as possible. Nita was only allowed an interval of two hours' sleep, after which they took a very early breakfast by starlight, although it was such dry work that it half-choked them, and their thirst had already got to be a dominant idea. Even so, it strengthened them for their journey, and they bravely set off again. In spite of these energetic measures and wise precautions, noon found the travellers still in the plain, which seemed like a lava-bed, still exposed to the terrific power of a sun such as we of more temperate climes can have no conception of; physically exhausted, suffering agonies of thirst, yet still moving on slowly. How their hearts had sunk as they watched that sun rise; with what dread had they seen it mount higher and higher; and how fully had all their expectations of evil been realized! The air they breathed seemed to scorch them, and was as hot and dry as though it had come from a furnace; the condition of the atmosphere was electrical, and it had the peculiar unbearable sultriness that precedes a thunder-storm; the earth seemed literally to steam and sent up a kind of mist through which everything looked ghostly and unnatural. If the children were still moving, it was because to stop for any length of time seemed to them to be courting and awaiting death.

All that morning they had not been able to walk more than five minutes without stopping to rest for ten, and, even so, Nita had to be aided by Juan, and Amigo required any amount of coaxing encouragement, since he sat down and panted certainly once to every hundred yards. The poor animal looked actually shrunken, and the misery in his bloodshot eyes so appealed to Nita that she shed tears over him repeatedly, although her own condition might have claimed all her sympathy. She embraced and caressed him, too, and evidently comforted him, for his whine was one of resignation, and his look full of fortitude and love as he licked her hands.

About four o'clock, during one of their halts, Juan was looking drearily before him, and thinking the most despairing thoughts, when all at once a moving object arrested his attention. It was so distant that it was a mere speck; but with the quickness and accuracy of vision that was partly natural to him, partly acquired, he soon made out that it was an antelope running across the plain. He knew it by its smooth, sheep-like gait, and continued to regard it with the interest that attaches to every living thing in the woods. He pointed it out to Nita, and told her what he thought of it. His voice sounded hollow and strange, and he spoke with great difficulty, his throat being swollen and parched.

Nita's eyes followed the direction indicated by his outstretched finger, and, while they were still looking at it, it suddenly loomed up in the air until it appeared as large as a camel, and then disappeared. Nita gave a hoarse scream, threw her arms around Juan's neck, hid her face on his shoulder, and trembled in every limb, and Juan, who would have faced any danger that he understood, was almost as much frightened. Yet they had nothing to fear, at least in that quarter, for this was the fantastic effect of mirage. Not knowing this, Juan was infinitely surprised and delighted, about half an hour later, to see a beautiful distant lake on his right. How it sparkled in the sun! With what passionate eagerness he seized Nita's hand and drew her toward it! They could see it plainly, set like a great jewel in the plain, the very ripples in it, with the rushes and sedges that grew along the margin reflected in it as in a mirror, the trees that grew beside, the white cranes standing in it.

In a frenzy of hope they first hurried, then
hobbled on, and on, and on, until at last they
reached it. But, alas! alas! It was all a delusion,
or rather illusion, and if it was one to tempt and
tantalize a traveller under the most ordinary
circumstances, what was it to two perishing
children who had not had a drop of water for
thirty-six hours?

When Juan got up to it, and found only a
ravine and a few whitened bones, his disappointment was so intense that he threw himself down
on the earth with a loud, bitter cry, and could
only groan when Nita came up to him. One
thing she understood without explanation —
there was no water. Without a moan she dropped
down by him. The same thought was in the
minds of both. This was the end. There they
lay for a long while, and despair brought with it
calmness. 'Our poor mother!' said Nita in a
whisper; and then, seeing that tears were running down Juan's cheeks, she took his hand and
drew it up to her, saying, 'Poor Juan!' and closed
her eyes, nor ever expected to open them again.

But these dear children were not destined to
perish then or there. Before they set out for the
ravine, there was a small cloud in one part of the

heavens, that grew and extended in a way that must have attracted their notice had they not been absorbed in their quest of the lovely lake, and so, when succor seemed impossible, and hope had died out of their hearts, help was at hand, and came from the last quarter from which they would have expected it. Juan finally opened his eyes and looked at Nita. The sight of her lying there so white, haggard, altered, her breath coming in little labored gasps from between her parted lips, filled him with a new horror; and the remembrance of the patience with which she had borne all the agony and torment of the last two days wrung his heart with anguish. He thought she was dying. He could do nothing to help her. With a deep groan he turned away from her, and covered his face with his hands.

Juan's own exhaustion was so great that he lay in a sort of stupor for some time. He was dimly conscious that there had been some change going on, but whether it was darkness or death that was coming to him he could not have told. From this state he was roused by a peal of thunder that penetrated even to his veiled consciousness. He sat up dizzy and confused.

A flash of lightning lit up all the wide plain, but he only saw Nita's ghastly face, and, believing her to be dead, gave a shriek of utter despair, so hoarse and dreadful that it reached her, and filled her with alarm. Unclosing her eyes, she called Juan's name feebly, and he, transported by joy at finding her alive, took her in his arms and poured out the most incoherent and extravagant expressions of affection and encouragement.

And now he saw with kindling rapture that all the heavens were black above him and knew that they were saved. His mind cleared; he could act and think once more. He picked Nita up, and staggered with her down into the ravine. Looking down it he saw a place where the bank had been probably undermined at high water, and formed a kind of overhanging pent roof. Here he put his pack and the bows and returned to Nita.

For a few minutes they sat there with their faces turned up to the sky, thirsting with longing that cannot be conceived unless it has been felt for what was withheld. Then a sudden blast of wind swept down the ravine, whirling before it pebbles and sticks from the bed, cacti and bushes from the brink of the dead stream, and all at once down came the blessed, blessed rain! It fell in torrents; with positive fury it whipped and lashed the earth and rocks in exulting rage. Its violence was terrible; all the thunders of heaven seemed poured out in the air, all its lightnings stabbed the darkness and threatened the earth. It was magnificent, awful! But the children did not heed it, or dread it, or fly from it. They received it on their knees, with reverence and deepest gratitude as a Godsend, which it was. Their burning bodies were drenched by it; their burning lips and throats sucked it up greedily as it fell, and felt that they had never known what water was before; their scorched lungs drew in its sweet moisture, full of all healing; their very hearts and souls rejoiced and were glad!

When they had started off so eagerly to find the lake of the mirage, Amigo had refused to follow them. Perhaps he had reasons of his own for disbelieving in the existence of that body of water; perhaps he felt that he had already made too many concessions in the course of this dreadful pilgrimage, and was suffering accordingly; perhaps, like themselves, he was utterly worn out and sick at heart. But certainly, when Juan

called to him roughly to follow, he did nothing of
the sort. He lay down, looked all humble de-
precation and affection, wagged his tail in a
feebly apologetic way, but did not move. When
Juan went back, patted his head, and put the
case differently, he looked doubly humble,
deeply distressed, and even more affectionate,
while the play of his tail was almost lively, but he
had not altered his resolution. He put his head
down between his fore-paws as an ultimatum, and
positively refused to stir. So they left him there,
intending if he did not follow to return to him with
water, and later to coax him to return with them
to camp. After that Amigo was forgotten.

Late in the evening, when the storm which
had been so long gathering had spent itself in a
mighty outburst too violent to last, and left the
world that it found fainting under its trial by
fire, a sweet, cool, gray place, fit to be the home
of man, and bird, and beast, who should come
running up the ravine, yes, actually running,
and leap upon Juan and Nita with as much
effusion as though he had been separated from
them for a year, but Amigo, wonderfully revived and refreshed like themselves! It was a
joyous reunion.

The children thought that Amigo must distrust the water-supply of the region and wish to provide for possible emergencies in the future; for he was always breaking away from them and running down below to lap up a few mouthfuls and gaze reflectively at the swift little stream that was now rushing over the pebbled bed of the ravine. The water that the earth could not absorb had poured into this natural drain in such quantities that it had rapidly grown into a torrent. Juan feared it might reach and sweep away his precious pack and bow. He left Nita and went off to see how they fared, found the water within an inch of his wallet; scrutinized the rock about him, which, with its crevices, mosses, lichens and tufts of grass, enabled him to gauge pretty accurately the high-water mark of previous floods, seized his bow and hung it well above that line, and carried his pack back with him.

Juan spread his blanket on the ground, and he and Nita seated themselves on it. It made a nice carpet for them during supper, and a waterproof bed when sleepy-time came — a bed that Amigo graciously shared with them for fully ten hours.

And what a lovely world it was that they opened their eyes on next morning! As fresh as though it had just been created, and everything in it singing inaudibly for joy. How changed the aspect of nature! The very heavens seemed purified; the loveliest tints of unsuspected green had been brought to light all about them; every blade of grass, every leaf, had righted itself and held a dewdrop to its heart; the birds were pouring themselves out in an ecstasy of glad melody; earth, air, and sky were alike cool, calm, heavenly.

Its delicious tranquillity and beauty sank deep into the hearts of the children after the stormy emotions of the preceding day. They had suffered too keenly to be able to rejoice exactly; but it was happiness enough to be out of pain and danger, and they were full of quiet content. It almost seemed that they had only dreamed of that arid waste and cruel sun.

Nita looked so pale that Juan was uncertain whether to go on or call a halt. The noisy, impetuous stream that they had heard rushing off into darkness as they were falling asleep the night before had already dwindled to an ordinary brook, and Juan knew would soon disappear altogether. And, although the deep pools cut in

the bed of the ravine by the gravel and sand
washed down at flood-tide would give them water
for several days, Juan had a nervous dread of
trusting to these alone. He was afraid to stop
where there was no lasting supply of water, and
he was reminded at breakfast that there was not
much food left; so he determined to make a short
march, and, if possible, get shade for Nita before
noon. As they walked away, he noticed that,
whereas, on the previous day he had not seen a
single rabbit or squirrel, they seemed now to
have sprung out of the earth in mysterious
plentifulness, and were scampering around hunting water, in high glee. They had gone about
three miles when they came to a single fine oak
crowning a knoll; and, while Nita sat below
under the pleasant wide-spreading branches,
Juan climbed up into it and reconnoitred the
country. He was delighted to see a wood growing in the ribbon fashion that told of a stream,
and he calculated that it was not more than seven
miles distant. Other trees he saw too, like the
friendly one in which he was making these observations. Nita would be able to make the
journey by easy stages, and rest often.

Pleased with these discoveries, they chatted

cheerfully, and walked arm in arm together for about an hour, when Juan suddenly stopped, and said, 'Ki!' in an astonished tone. He slipped his arm out of Nita's, too, and walked off to the right, telling her to stay where she was. This command she ventured to disobey, and joining him in a moment found him staring fixedly at a long, shining line drawn across the wet prairie.

'What is it? What made it?' she asked eagerly, but got no response. Juan was following it. She followed him, and presently both came upon footprints and the marks of horses' hoofs. 'The Comanches!' exclaimed Nita, and turned livid with fright. Still no reply from Juan who had got down on the ground, and was all eyes.

'Made by a tent-pole,' he said at last, pointing to the serpentine trail that had first attracted his attention. 'Made since the rain. Indians, but not Comanches, I think. A hunting-party. Look at this. Blood! It has probably dropped from dead game. Seven of them are mounted men, and three walked, of whom one was lame, and has hurt himself recently, for he threw the whole weight of his body on the right foot as far as possible. They have gone to that river.'

'Oh, let us go back! Come! Come, Juan!'

cried out Nita, and began to run in the opposite direction from that taken by the unknown travellers.

'Stop, Nita, stop!' called out Juan; but Nita would not stop. She had Casteel for a motive-power, and got over so much ground that Juan was put to it to overtake her.

When he seized her by the arm, she cried out, angrily:

'Why do you stop me? Let us fly back to the ravine as fast as we can.'

'Oh, no! — that won't do, Nita. We can't go back there,' he said.

'Then where shall we go?' she asked.

'We shall have to get to water,' he said. 'There will be no water there where we came from by to-morrow, perhaps — at best in a few days it will all be gone — and we must have food, too. Let me think.' He did think, and soon gave the conclusion he had reached. 'When you set an old hound on wolves, he always takes the back track, Casteel says. That's what I am going to do. They are going to camp with the game they have killed. They won't turn back. We shall be safer behind them than anywhere else if we don't get too close. I shall follow their trail until we get near the river, and then I'll reconnoitre and see what I can see, and what we had best do. Come on.'

'Oh, Juan — dearest Juan! Don't do that. You must be mad to think of it,' Nita expostulated. 'They will be sure to find us, and kill us. Oh, do, *do*, DO come back to the ravine or go somewhere, anywhere else except to the river!'

A brother who threw himself in the teeth of an enemy, jumped down his very throat, as it were, at one time, and stuck to his heels at another, was a brother that Nita could not understand at all. So she wept, and sobbed, and urged instant flight; and Juan waited patiently until her tears and terrors were somewhat abated, and then he explained again his views and intentions kindly and affectionately, and, at last, Nita, unconvinced but conquered, yielded. She shivered and looked back; she shivered and looked forward; she started at the sound of Juan's voice, and trembled at her own shadow. She stopped occasionally, and reopened the question as to whether they should go on or go back; but Juan went on, and she, with many a sigh, followed. She had no other choice.

About a mile from the river Juan stopped.

'We will take our dinner under this oak,' he said. 'If any one comes this way we can climb up into it. If no one comes we will stay until dark allows us to go nearer. I noticed early this morning that all the game we came upon was very wild. I could not understand it then. These Indians have been here for some weeks, I think. The party whose tracks we saw this morning have been off hunting a long way from here, otherwise they would not be going back to camp at this hour of the day. They will feel quite secure and will not be on the lookout for us. I think if we are careful we can creep right up on them to-night.' Juan's eyes sparkled at the idea, and he seemed to be regarding it as a great treat in store for both.

But Nita took quite another view of it. 'I can't go that near, Juan. I can't, indeed. I won't! I wouldn't for anything in the world creep up on Casteel. He would see me. No woods could hide me from him. I hate him!' she said rapidly, with a shudder of recollection as that mirage presented itself to her mind.

'Very well, Nita. You can stay somewhere while I go. I don't believe they are Comanches; but I must find out,' said Juan.

Nita was willing to take a great deal for granted where Indians were concerned, and had no desire to make further investigation; but she knew it was useless to attempt to dissuade Juan. She had but small appetite for their dinner and was a prey to the most distressing anxieties. Suppose Juan should be killed or captured and she left alone in the woods? What if they were to be carried off by a strange tribe to another mountain fastness from which it would be impossible to escape? The idea of being reënslaved, now that she had tasted the sweetness of liberty and was full of hope for the future, was quite unbearable, and brought out a last 'Do turn back, Juan! We may as well die of thirst as to be recaptured, perhaps killed.'

'Oh, we are not caught yet!' he coolly replied; and she wondered to see him eat his noonday meal as unconcernedly as though he was taking it at the *hacienda*. He seemed to be ravenously hungry and could have devoured all the food they had, but prudently left two small pieces of turkey for their supper.

When dusk came, and they could travel across the open stretch of prairie that separated the timber in which they were hiding from the woods that fringed the river, Juan and Nita walked swiftly toward the point of entrance he had selected. Having secured the shelter afforded by the strip of forest, Juan parted the interlacing boughs of some tall *fijal* bushes, and signed Nita to enter. She obeyed; Amigo followed her; Juan let the boughs swing back into place. The child and dog were completely hidden; and, satisfied of this, Juan stood still for a moment and looked about him and above him, fixing certain points in his mind. He was starting off with his own light, quick, noiseless step, when he looked around and saw that Amigo had popped out of his leafy covert, and was following him. He also heard a low, plaintive 'Oh, Juan, don't leave me!' from Nita.

'Go back, sir — go back!' he said to Amigo, who looked up into his face with an expression of mild but settled obstinacy, varied by one of lively inquiry that said, 'What on earth are you up to now, I should like to know?' Amigo paid no heed to a second command. Juan picked up a stone. Amigo turned tail and would have fled. He had an objection to being shut up in out-of-the-way places when there was good sport to be had. But Juan seized him roughly by the neck, and half led, half kicked him into the very lap of Nita, who was seated on the ground. She received him with open arms, and soon reconciled him to the situation by her caresses, and as for Juan, he was off that instant, only stopping to say, 'Be quiet. Don't move about. I'll not be long.'

How long Nita stayed crouched down in the midst of the bushes while Juan was crawling, wriggling, gliding, sliding along on his way to the camp as only a snake and an Indian can, she never knew. It seemed to her, in her terror and loneliness, half the night. It was probably about two hours. But at last, when she had almost despaired of ever seeing him again, he returned, slipped into her hiding-place, clapped a hand over Amigo's mouth when he would have barked, and gave an account of his expedition.

'Indians, as I thought,' he said; 'but not Comanches. Lipans, I know, for I found this [holding up an arrow]. They always feather and paint them like this. Casteel has got the arrows of every tribe for five hundred miles, and I knew it was a Lipan arrow the moment I saw it. They are camped about a half-mile distant, not far from the river. It is an old camp, and they have been there for at least two moons. They have killed and dried the greatest quantity of meat, and I think they will break camp soon, and go on the war-path. They were restringing their bows and straightening their arrows. There are about seventy-five warriors, almost all young, and I stole this from under their very noses.' Juan laughed quietly with carefully suppressed amusement as he spoke, and held out for inspection a long strip of jerked venison. 'They are so busy with their preparations for the expedition they have planned, whatever it is, that they will not straggle about much. They will stick to their camp, I think. But we are a little too close to them.'

'Oh, yes! we are entirely too close,' agreed Nita, who would have liked to be a thousand miles away.

'We will drop down below here a little, near the river,' said Juan. 'Do you smell anything? The stench from the offal they have thrown out almost knocked me down. It seems to me that I can still smell it.'

'Yes, it is dreadful. Let us get away farther,' said Nita, anxious to leave the neighborhood on any pretext.

'We need a good rest, and I am going to take it,' said Juan. 'In two or three days they will be off, and then we can stay as long as we please.'

'Two or three days? Oh, Juan!' replied Nita, to whom this sounded like two or three months.

'Well, I don't know,' said Juan. 'To-morrow, perhaps. Don't be scared. I will keep well out of their way; trust me for that. We mustn't eat anything to-night, and as little as possible to-morrow. I don't know where we are going to get any more, you know, with seventy-five Indians around, and —'

'Oh, Juan, there is that smell again! Do let us be off,' said Nita anxiously, rising to her feet at the mention of the warriors.

There was no rest for Nita that night. Juan stopped at a place where the undergrowth was thickly crowning a bold cliff above the river, and pointed to a small grass-covered mound, saying, 'There is a nice little bed for you, *hermanita mia*, all made up, and quite ready. Let us take a plunge in the river before we go to sleep.'

But Nita was afraid the sound of splashing water would be overheard by some stray Indian, and denied herself the bath that night that might have soothed and refreshed her over-tired, over-excited frame, and induced sleep. She slipped down to the river-side, indeed, but it was only to slake her thirst; and all that night she lay awake, listening to the musical ripple of the water as it ran over a ledge of rock near by, dreading all possible and impossible evils.

The river, however, as it flowed past the Indian camp told no tales about two children on a cliff; the night wind wandered from tree to tree and learned the secrets of every leaf, but kept its own counsel; the stars which once led good men to where a young child lay, were not the stars to betray this brother and sister to evil ones, and, often forced to hide wicked men and deeds, were only too glad to guard the innocent, and so no harm came to Juan and Juanita.

CHAPTER VII

THE CAÑON OF ROSES

Even Juan did not dare to approach the Indian camp by daylight, and he and Nita remained concealed on the cliff all the next day until it was quite dark. Juan made one or two pilgrimages to the river for water to wash down the dried meat that would otherwise have stuck in their throats; but that was all, and even these brief absences gave Nita the most serious uneasiness.

It was weary work waiting for the hours to pass, especially to children accustomed to a large liberty of action and the most active exercise; but there was no help for it; and as for Amigo, he was disgusted to find himself in fault, no matter what he did. The friendliest bark or whine seemed to be misinterpreted; an innocent frisk, gambol, or growl was instantly suppressed; and every little diversion in the way of running into the bushes got him into trouble. It was quite inexplicable to a dog tolerably well used, he thought, to the senseless vagaries of human-kind, and he waxed quite sulky at last, curled himself up at Nita's feet, and looked aggrieved

inquiry from under his wrinkled eyebrows at a
capricious mistress and disagreeable master. It
was not until Juan had taken himself off at
evening to find out what the Indians were doing,
and Nita showed some appreciation of his services
as a faithful and devoted friend by putting one
arm around his neck and confiding to him that
she was lonely and frightened, that Amigo
weakly relented, and became his usual forgiving,
loving, slobbering self.

Juan got back sooner than she expected, and
seemed well satisfied with his observations.

'They are all packed and ready to start; they
will be off before daylight to-morrow morning,
you will see,' he announced, cheerfully; and he
was not mistaken.

While it was still dark he climbed to the top of
a great oak that commanded an extensive view
of the surrounding country, and smiled, well
pleased, when he saw the enemy file slowly out of
the woods, their slouching figures dimly visible
in the uncertain light, the whole company a black
dot on the plain for a time, and then two black
dots, as after a halt they separated, one party
turning their faces to the south, the other toward
the northwest. Juan was shouting and laughing

so joyously and triumphantly when he came
scrambling up the side of the cliff that he awoke
Nita from a sound sleep, and gave her a fright
lest she should have been discovered by her
dreaded enemies.

'Gone! Gone! All gone!' sang out Juan. 'And
now come along! Don't stay here another minute.
I have seen them off from my perch near their
camp, and they will not be back here for many
a day. They have sent the old men and the
greater part of the provisions home, and the
others have evidently gone off on a raid — perhaps against the Texicanos.'

'Poor things, I pity them! I wonder, Juan,
what our mother is doing this morning,' said
Nita, her thoughts reverting to the Comanche
raid in which she had been captured, and then to
her mother.

'Eating her breakfast, most likely,' replied
Juan, 'and that is what we had better be doing,
if we can find one.'

Moved by an impulse of natural curiosity, they
went at once to the deserted camp. Nita's pretty
little nose went up higher and higher as they approached it; and, certainly, if a smell could have
guarded a camp the Lipans would have had

nothing to fear from their bitterest foes. The children found only the remains of a fire, the scaffolding on which the meat had been dried, and, scattered on the ground, a few handfuls of corn, which they eagerly picked up. They were glad enough to get away from the place; and, fortunately, just as they were leaving, Juan spied a strip of venison, that had been overlooked, hanging from a cross-pole.

When they returned to the river, Juan exclaimed, 'Now that we can build a fire, I'll catch some fish. If the Indians see the smoke they will think their own campfire has caught some dry wood and blazed up; but I'll not make more than is necessary. Where is the pack?'

The next moment Juan was calling on the saints in true Mexican fashion; for, on examining the pack, Juan found everything except what he most needed and had counted on. The fishing-tackle that he had so ingeniously constructed was nowhere to be found! It had been forgotten and left behind in a corner of the cave; and the children almost quarrelled in the eagerness with which each tried to prove that it was the fault of the other. But the fact remained; and another fact was equally certain — the tackle could not be duplicated. So they could only make the best of a bad situation, and sat down on the river's bank, under the shade of a group of grand old oaks, and ate slowly and sparingly of the dry corn and drier meat that not all the water at hand could make very palatable.

The children were further aggravated by the behavior of the fish below them; which, as if fully understanding what had happened, would swim lazily around and about the roots of a willow that overhung the stream, bump their noses against the bank, and eye the children impudently, as if to say, 'Oh! you are there, are you? Why don't you come and catch us, pray?' and then swim lazily away again. When Juan threw in little sticks, they would rush for them just as if they wished to show him what he could do if he only had bait instead, on the end of a hook attached to a line.

At last he could stand it no longer. He could not fish, but he could shoot. Together the children tramped over many a mile that day, but were never able to get near enough to anything to get a shot. The game they saw fled before them, and it was with great difficulty that, with Amigo's help, Juan got one rabbit late in the afternoon.

'Oh, dear, when we get food, we never have any water; and when we get water, the food always gives out,' complained Nita.

'There is no use in our staying here. We should starve. The Indians have been here too long. We will start off again this evening,' said Juan, disappointed of the rest and comfort he had expected, anxious to linger near the river, yet afraid to do so.

With the fixed idea of reaching Mexico, Juan took his bearings afresh, and crossed the river before dark, facing southwest. That evening the children walked eight miles and slept in the open prairie.

All the next day they trudged along patiently under a hot sun with but scanty refreshment, and lively fears lest some of their previous experiences should be repeated. The day after, they began to suffer again from the old heat and thirst and hunger, the old weariness and depression. At the close of that day they gnawed eagerly at the one bone left from their rabbit. It was then given to Amigo who ground it to powder with his strong white teeth and stood at 'attention,' waiting for more. They had kept a sharp lookout for something to eat; but the game was still unapproachable. They were so hungry that they could not go to sleep for the gnawing pain they were enduring, and Juan dug up some roots with which to satisfy this craving.

At last, overcome by their great weariness, they dropped off to troubled slumbers and awoke to another ten hours of varied and acute physical misery. Happily, Juan had found at the camp an old leathern bottle, which had been discarded or forgotten by the Indians, and this he had filled at the river. It saved them much suffering; but a diet of roots and tepid water is not the most strengthening in the world. They were limping wearily along over a high plateau, across which they had been travelling for two days, when suddenly they were brought up with a short turn by finding themselves on the very brink of a precipice.

Looking across a wide chasm, they could see a sheer wall of rock on the other side extending indefinitely below, on either hand, and beyond that a continuation of the plateau. Loud were their exclamations; great their surprise. But while Nita saw in it only an insuperable obstacle to further progress, to Juan it brought renewed animation and hope. Peering over the side as fearlessly as though he were a chamois, Juan made out, through the shadows that were already gathering in the lower part of the cañon, a beautiful little river at the bottom imprisoned between the stern rocks that shut out everything except heaven, yet going quietly on its shining way, brightening and refreshing that secluded spot as some brave souls do the gloomy places of earth, seen only of God.

The sinking sun sent beautiful oblique shafts of light down into the opening, and several flocks of doves wheeled above it. 'I wish we could drop down there as easily as they can,' said Juan, pointing to them, 'but we must get there somehow, and before night too.'

'I have often wished for wings,' replied Nita. 'It would be delightful to fly away up yonder, and then drop right down like a stone.'

'If we are quick about it, we may get some game at once,' said Juan, paying no attention to her remark, his thoughts full of more practical matters. 'There is always a chance of it where there is water. Come on! If there are any deer about, I must get down before they have all had water, and gone out into the hills again.'

He took another look into and along the abyss,

to see if there was anything that indicated a break in its surface, and, finding nothing, he started off at random along the brink. By a most fortunate chance — if it was chance — he had come upon the cañon not a quarter of a mile from an intersecting, tortuous ravine, the only entrance to it from that side in a distance of fifteen miles. There was an opening on the opposite side about three miles below; but that would have been of small benefit to him while that chasm yawned between.

Juan knew very well that it was only a chance whether he should find an opening that night or a week later; so it was no wonder that he gave vent to a shout of delight when he came to a deep ravine, cleft in the plateau by some such convulsion of nature as had created the cañon, thickly filled with dwarf-oaks and pines and undergrowth, and with a distinct trail running down it, made by game of different kinds.

'Lots of deer and turkeys must come to this place,' he cried. 'Just look at the tracks. How thick they are, and coming in from every direction. Hurrah! Here we go!'

Tired as they both were, they were so inspired by the thought of getting food that they fairly ran down the ravine for some distance. The descent was not an easy one by any means, extremely steep in some places, gradual in others, and apparently interminable. It seemed to Nita that they were descending into the very bowels of the earth, and their clothes were torn again and again; their faces and hands were scratched by the long, sharp mesquite thorns until they bled; they walked over beds of cacti sometimes, picking their way as best they could; and once Juan stumbled headlong over some rocks, so eager was he to reach the river.

Twice Nita grew dizzy, and had to be guided by Juan along a narrow ledge that skirted the rock, with her eyes either shut or fixed on the sky above her. The sight of the depths below was more than she could bear. At last they got on level ground, and found that what had looked like a very narrow strip of ground, when seen from the plateau, had widened out into quite a little valley, as green and fresh as possible, having one most beautiful feature that had given it the name, among both the Indians and white men, of the 'Cañon of Roses.'

How the flowers came to grow there no one could say; but there they were, running up to the very edge of the cliffs, mantling the face of the rock for hundreds of yards, blooming in inconceivable profusion and beauty, perfuming all the air, throwing out myriads of tendrils full of prodigal promise in folded bud and leaf — an exquisite sight! Little short-breathed cries of '*Linda! Hermosa! Magnifica!*' ('Beautiful! Lovely! Magnificent!') went up from Juan and Juanita, as they sank panting on the earth. Unaccustomed as they were to noticing such things, they could not but be struck by the loveliness of the place. It seemed a little heaven to them, with its sweet flowers and grass, its trees and river, its coolness and delicious odors, its soft light and growing shadows. After the heat and glare and misery of that journey over the plateau it seemed enough joy merely to look and live with such surroundings. But hunger is an importunate creditor and cannot long be put off.

'The evening is drawing down, and the game will be coming in soon,' said Juan, when his thoughts reverted to the great question of food. 'We will hide now.'

Nita agreed to this. They rose, sought out and carefully concealed themselves behind some bushes near the plainest trail, and had hardly

done so when several fine old bucks came trotting
fearlessly up the valley, and went down into the
river; but on the opposite side. The sight of
them excited Juan tremendously. What if he
should be on the wrong side of the stream?
Should he swim across it and conceal himself
over there? Then, remembering the unmistakable evidences afforded by the deer-run he was
guarding, and rightly concluding that there was
an opening into the cañon on the opposite side
that might be investigated later, he kept perfectly still and quiet. The next moment he heard
a little metallic clink of hoofs against the rock,
and then a slight cough. His heart bounded, and
beat almost to suffocation. Looking around, he
and Nita saw an old doe and two beautiful little
spotted fawns coming directly down the trail
they were watching.

The children scarcely dared to breathe. The
wind was blowing away from the deer; and the
doe, scenting no danger, came on, followed by
her pretty innocents, until she got nearly opposite the young hunters, and very near them.
Juan promptly decided to shoot the doe, and
then try afterwards to get the fawns, which he
knew would be apt to linger near their mother.

Accordingly, just as the doe got beyond him, he rose to shoot. But he could not do it! He could not so much as take aim. He trembled so violently that his arrow bobbed irresolutely up and down as if in a convulsion, nor could he steady it. His knees fairly knocked together; and, although he made the most violent efforts to control himself, he could not succeed. He held his breath so long that it was a wonder he didn't break a blood-vessel. He set his teeth; he was furious with himself; but for the life of him he could not shoot!

It was no feeling of compassion for the creatures before him that unnerved him, although they might very well have appealed to his heart; it was not that he was overcome by all that he had lately undergone; it was simply that he was suffering from an acute attack of 'buck ague.'

This is a disease that all men with a passion for field sports have felt. Those who have never known it have never fully enjoyed hunting; but the worst of it is that it always makes its appearance at the wrong time. Juan had never experienced it before, and could not imagine what was the matter with him. He kept pointing at the motherly old doe until she had quite passed by, and then he tried feebly to aim at each of the fawns; but all in vain. He was so weak that he had to sit down, Nita staring at him all the while in mute but intense astonishment.

'Are you ill?' she whispered, finally, alarmed by his appearance and behavior.

'Keep still,' whispered Juan in return. 'Keep still!' He then set to work in earnest to conquer himself. He put his bow down, drew a long breath, and gave himself a severe lecture, in this wise: 'You ninny! why are you trembling and shaking so? You couldn't hit the side of a mountain, much less a deer, in your present state. And what if you do miss? It isn't the only deer in the world. Steady yourself, and be cool now, and take good aim.'

Meanwhile the doe and her little ones had gone down into the river; and a lovely picture they made as they stood there; the mother dignified, gentle, protecting; now moving about gracefully in the clear stream; now stopping and glancing about her, as if to make sure that all was well, and her children in no danger; now stretching her neck down and letting the water ripple into her mouth; and ever casting looks of tender, contented love on the fawns as they frisked about and drank, and gave playful little bounds and leaps here and there, all joy and innocent beauty. The whole group ought first to have been transferred to one of Landseer's canvases, and then to an animal paradise of perennial grass, limpid waters, and perfect peace. But, alas! Juan was himself again. His bow no longer trembled; the arrow had been carefully chosen and fitted into place.

The river episode was the pleasantest of the day to the fawns, and they were in no hurry to end it; but the doe, seeing that they had drunk their fill, and that it was getting late, exerted her authority, and finally succeeded in leading them up the green bank again. Here in a moment she caught scent of the children, and came on slowly, stepping very high, with head and tail erect, her whole expression one of uneasy alertness. Her great soft eyes roved anxiously from point to point, until at last they rested on Juan; while the fawns trotted along at her heels in happy ignorance of such things as enemies or arrows.

It was Nita who secured for the party a brief respite. Eager to see what was passing, she rose on her knees just at the moment that Juan was about to shoot, and accidentally jogged his elbow as he let his arrow fly. The doe had not had time fully to make out what Juan was. The arrow passed over her back, and she wheeled and ran in the direction it had taken. It struck a dead tree and knocked down a large piece of bark, which fell in front of the doe, and she wheeled back toward the children, confused, and uncertain where the danger lay. She stopped so near them that they could hear her breathing, and then walked back to where the bark had fallen.

The moment had come. Juan, whose nerves were now entirely under control, took aim at her heart, and let drive his shaft. The doe sprang high into the air, and ran off with outstretched neck, her tail whipping from side to side, a deadly fear for her fawns at her heart, more agonizing than the arrow that had given her a mortal wound. The frightened fawns followed close at her heels, carrying their white flags high in air. Suddenly the doe fell, turning a complete somersault. Finding their progress thus arrested, the fawns bounded lightly over her, frisked playfully on for a little distance, and then turned and walked back. Astonished, apparently, to find their mother still lying there, and much puzzled by her curious behavior of the last few minutes, they put their little noses down to her, as if in this way to discover the trouble, whatever it was. Just then the doe gave a desperate, dying kick with both hind feet that threw the torn-up grass and leaves into the faces of the fawns, and, drawing a deep, guttural breath at the same moment that frightened them out of their wits, died to them and a cruel world.

The fawns tumbled back over each other in utter consternation. Never had their mother behaved in such a way; and, as if for explanation, they ran right toward the children, who were advancing to secure their prize. When they came quite close, they received one that even they understood. Juanita's bow was also strung, and she was anxious for a shot, so she took good aim and sent an arrow deep into the side of one of the fawns; Juan also shot and struck the same one. Bleating most pitifully, it ran off down the valley, followed by its frightened little companion, Amigo at their heels, convinced that he had caught a deer, and could hunt as well as some other people. Juan followed, and when the fawn fell, seized it, and dragged it back to a place near his camp. Satisfied with the food in hand, he had allowed the second fawn to escape, and now seized his knife and fell to butchering the doe, while Nita got wood for the fire.

The change from an empty wallet to an abundance of good meat was a cheering one; and, untroubled by sentimental regret, Juan's eyes glistened greedily as he cut piece after piece from the doe, which was in excellent condition, and from the fat little fawn. These he strung, a bit of lean and a bit of fat alternately, on a pole sharpened at both ends, and carried it over to the camp, unable to think of the future until his present longing was satisfied.

Nita had a hot fire ready, and with a vigorous thrust he stuck one end of the pole in the ground before the blaze. The venison soon began to give out the most savory odors; and, as the children heard the fat hissing and sputtering, and saw the juices running out of the meat, they gave vent to a great many exclamations, expressive of the liveliest satisfaction and pleasantest anticipations. They watched it growing browner and browner, they could hardly wait for it to cook; and the very instant it was done, Juan stretched out his hand to seize the pole, and actually had it in his grasp, when a tremendous uproar reached his ears, causing him to replace it hastily.

The noise sounded like that made by horses' feet in running, then followed a few short yelps, and then Amigo rushed into camp with five or six wolves at his heels. He had been left to guard the meat at the place where it had been butchered, but the coyotes had smelt the blood, and invited themselves to supper. Amigo, finding the odds too great, had fled and been pursued, and here they all were, dog and wolves, growling, snarling, howling terrifically, not a dozen yards away! The din and the suddenness of the onset frightened Nita so dreadfully that she ran away as fast as her legs could carry her! Great was her horror of wolves at any time; and it was not surprising that she could not face a pack of them at a moment's notice.

Juan, however, had been growing more self-reliant every day since he left the Comanche camp, and stood his ground bravely. Quick as thought he seized a brand from the fire and thrust it among the wolves. Not expecting an attack at all, much less one of such a startling nature, they shrank back, cowed, and slunk off, with the exception of one large coyote who had a score to settle with Amigo, and continued to chase him. Dropping the brand, Juan sent an arrow into his side. He fell over and yelled, and then, jumping up, tore up the valley, with Amigo no longer the pursued but the pursuer. Juan followed and heard a loud snapping and barking, which told him that they were fighting, and made him hasten to Amigo's aid. When he got up to them, though, it was clear that Amigo needed no allies. The wolf was in the agonies of death, and Amigo was holding him down by the throat, with a look of savage exultation on his face that was almost human, or rather quite diabolical. Juan called him off, and patted his head and praised him. The wolf was dragged back to camp, where Amigo sniffed at him more than once, contemptuously enough, during the evening. Nita had returned, and was, of course, complimented on her bravery by Juan. She retaliated by asking who had sat shivering and trembling behind the bushes, that very day, in an ague-fit worse than hers. Both remembered that they had had nothing to eat yet, and the next moment they were seated on the ground, and seized a rib apiece of the defunct doe, which claimed and received all their attention. Of the yard of venison cooked, there was not enough left for Amigo, and the ribs were picked as clean

as possible besides, so ravenously hungry were
the hunters.

It must not be supposed, though, that Amigo
was allowed to lack for anything after his heroic
defence of his master's property. On the contrary, he made a most enormous supper off the
carcasses of the deer, and swelled as visibly in
the process as though he had been a kitten before
a saucer of milk. This done, he walked about
with a portly, well-satisfied air, like a dog on
good terms with himself, conscious within well-
bred limits of his exceptional merits. And then
he stretched himself out comfortably near the
fire, with all the affability and simplicity of the
truly great, as much as to say, 'Observe me! I
catch a deer and kill a wolf on the same day, and
then I retire modestly into private life as if nothing had happened.' He fell asleep in this admirable frame of mind, and the children were not
long in following his distinguished example.

Juan built up the fire before he lay down for
the night, and began the process of 'jerking'
meat by putting some of it on a little scaffold of
green boughs well above the flame; but he was
too tired to do much. During the night they
were several times wakened by the whistling of

the deer that came down to water; and Juan, more than half asleep, would get up, mechanically turn over the meat, renew the fire, and drop down again by Nita's side.

Nita thought the wolves were upon them each time, and would have kept awake if it had been possible; but her great weariness always got the better of her fears. Guarded by Juan and Amigo on the right and left, she slept profoundly. But there was no rest for a certain little fawn which wandered up and down the valley all the night long, seeking the mother it had lost, wandering it knew not where, bleating plaintively in the darkness — a most unhappy dear little deer.

CHAPTER VIII

ESTRELLA

A MORE cool, lovely, fragrant spot than the Cañon of Roses, in the dewy hush of early morning, one could hardly find the world over; and a joyous awakening was that of the children. Comfortably secure of a breakfast, they set Amigo to guard their meat, and went off for a walk up the valley, in order to get some idea of their surroundings. The valley alternately narrowed and broadened as they ascended it, so that at times there was but a path between the gray, lichen-dotted wall of rock on one hand and the river on the other, while at others there was quite a stretch of greensward between the two, almost a meadow, with trees that might have shown for what they were had they been upon the plateau — of respectable, if not extraordinary, proportions — but so dwarfed by their surroundings that they looked like large bushes until you got up to them, and so had another standard of measurement than the one afforded by the walls of the cañon. In the open spaces there were wild flowers in great variety, some of them peculiar to that cañon. Ferns abounded also; and Nita soon had a bouquet, in which a great tuft of the white feather-plant was surrounded by other flowers of every color and most delicate loveliness. Juan was peering into every snake-hole, noticing every bubble on the water made by the fish, capturing insects, throwing stones, breaking off sticks with which to switch off the heads of flowers or grasses, nosing out a rabbit-warren, staring at game-tracks, plucking berries, chewing bits of bark or roots.

The river alone was full of attractions for both. Nita, free to obey her impulses, waded into it, as a matter of course, to get some lilies growing and blowing in one place so luxuriantly that the stream was almost bridged by a solid mass of floating, overlapping, shining leaves of darkest green, with lily matrons and lily-pod girls in white and gold walking across in beautiful procession. Juan sailed a whole fleet of wooden boats, or rather bits of wood, on it for quite an hour. They walked beside it for some distance, swam across it, wandered on the other side, until they were tired, and then returned to that on which they had camped, by a shallow spot where some white light was imprisoned even at that early hour, although all the stream was clouded, overshadowed like a mountain-tarn, giving out only steely-bluish, blackish surfaces as it rippled musically, eddied gently, or rushed boldly away in the soft gloom of the cañon. The coolest, quietest river imaginable at its brightest and noisiest — reflecting at midday, in a dim and distant fashion, the strip of sky overhead, or perhaps some great white cloud-Alp, as a metal mirror might have done.

When the children had finished dashing the water up into each other's faces to their mutual delight, they suddenly spied some brilliantly colored pebbles nestling together at the bottom of the stream, where there was a little stretch of shallow water; and, pleased with the pretty stones which looked like so many crown jewels, seen through the doubly purifying medium of a child's eye and clear water, the explorers seated themselves on the bank in such a way as to allow their feet to dangle comfortably in the water, and then fell to playing odd and even, their zest in the game being much heightened by the plashing pedal accompaniment they kept up all the while. They then threw themselves back on the grass, and stared up at the sky, and went on laughing and talking gleefully until a little rustle in the bushes near them attracted their attention and sent them up into a sitting posture at once.

Juan was alarmed, for he had thoughtlessly left his bow at the camp; but he had no need to be frightened; for now came a plaintive 'bleat, bleat, bleat,' and out came the little fawn they had spared the evening before. It was alone, and was still wandering about in an aimless, anxious way, trying to find out what had become of its family and friends. It had strayed down to the river to seek them, and, coming upon the children, stopped, and looked at them in a gentle, timid fashion, as if to say: 'Could you, would you, tell me, if you please, where my mother is? I am so tired, and I have looked everywhere. I don't know what to do, or where to go; I don't, indeed.'

'Oh, if I only had my bow!' said Juan. 'We need another bag to put honey in, and the skin of this fawn would make a splendid one, quite as big as the one Shaneco keeps bear's-oil in. What was I thinking of to come away without my bow? I tell you what; suppose we drive it very gently to our camp, and kill it there. You can do it if you like. But you must take good aim, and shoot at

the throat so as not to spoil the skin. I'll dress
it afterwards, and then make the bag.'

'Oh, poor little thing! Don't kill it, Juan,'
said Nita. 'It looks so helpless and frightened.
Let us keep it for a pet, if we can tame it.'

'Why, what nonsense!' he exclaimed. 'Of
course I shall kill it. But come on, I am hungry.
I want my breakfast.'

Together they managed to make the fawn
take the direction of the camp, and Juan dressed
its spotted skin all the way back in imagination.
But the longer Nita saw it and watched its
graceful movements, as it trotted or bounded
before them, the more pleased she was with its
slender legs, its comical apology for a tail, its
pretty coat, and the soft brilliancy of its eyes.
Every moment she grew more determined to
keep it. 'It is such a dear little thing. I must
have it; but how can I prevent Juan from killing
it?' she thought.

When they got near the camp, he bade her run
and fetch her bow or his; but she was ready with
an excuse. The fawn would not stray; it would
stay in the neighborhood; why not wait until
after breakfast? This seemed reasonable enough,
and Juan consented to postpone the shooting.

A very hearty breakfast put him in a good humor; and, indisposed to exert himself at all, he sat down on the river-bank with Nita, and spent an hour there in idleness. Then he all at once caught sight of a bee, that was sipping and fluttering just below him, and said, excitedly, 'See that! There's another! Plenty of honey about here somewhere. We must look for it. Now we've got the bag and the honey both.'

'Perhaps there isn't any honey down here at all. Let us look first, anyway, and then if we really find it —' said Nita.

Up jumped Juan, and started off with Nita to look for honey, having previously marked the direction the bees took when they left the river. His sharp eyes were soon looking not only at, but into, above, around the trees and cliffs as they went along, with the trained perception of a person who has been taught to use his eyes, not with the careless, unregarding, unobservant gaze that looks, indeed, but sees little or nothing.

Once Nita clapped her hands with joy, thinking she had found a bee-tree; but, on coming up, Juan said, 'Wasps, only wasps, Nita. You see a bee in every butterfly,' in rather a patronizing way. Soon after he caught a flash of something yellow flying in and out of the bottom of a tree, and cried out, 'Here! Here!' as he ran forward; but it was only a colony of yellow-jackets; and now it was Nita's turn to ask who was seeing bees in butterflies?

They walked on for some time after this, down the valley, Juan puzzled, eager, quite aggrieved that there was no honey to be found, Nita insisting that there was none to find, and that they had better go back to camp, when all at once they dipped down into a little gully, and came upon a dwarf post-oak leaning over it, about which bees, unmistakable bees, were flying in considerable numbers. It was evidently an 'At home,' a crowded apiarian reception, to which all the respectable bees of the neighborhood had been invited; and never was there a tree better adapted to social purposes of the kind, for it was a mere shell — an immense apartment tastefully fitted up and crowded with guests. A bear had gnawed quite a hole in it, and had doubtless tried to join in the festivities held there; but, being an uninvited guest and unwelcome, the intruder had been so rudely received, that, stung by their gibes and thrusts, he had left them to their own devices. But this had happened at some previous merry-making a long while before; for Juan noticed at once that the marks made by his teeth had nearly grown up. There had doubtless been other assaults; but the garrison was so numerous and so valiant that they had held their own against all their enemies.

'It is an old tree; and look how yellow with wax this hole is where the bees go in. There must be an immense store of honey, and some other people have found that out,' Juan said, as he laughingly pointed out the place where Bruin had left his card on the bark. 'We have no axe, nor hatchet. What shall we do? We must have that honey; that is certain. Let me think a moment.'

Dropping on the ground, Juan looked long and attentively at the oak, and Nita prattled away at his side, offering all sorts of suggestions, none of them very valuable ones, it must be confessed. Suddenly his eyes sparkled. He jumped to his feet and cried out, 'Hurrah! I've got it! We can't cut it down, but we can *burn* it down. Leaning, as it does, over the gully, the top will be sure to strike the opposite bank when it falls, and break the tree right off where the hive is. You'll see how it works, Nita. Run and get some wood.'

Off they both darted, seized an armful of dry
sticks apiece, brought it back, and piled it around
the roots of the oak, got another, and another,
until they had almost enough material for a bon-
fire, and more than enough for their purpose,
they thought, struck a light, and lo! a famous
blaze. The bees, accustomed to an easy-going
and sure-returning life, lulled by long security,
convinced of the impregnability of their position,
were utterly paralyzed, amazed, confounded by
this attack. They swarmed out of the hive when
the smoke reached them; they swarmed back
again, in the most intense state of excitement;
they could not see where to go, or whom to sting;
they buzzed out their anger and terror, and were
utterly distracted; and all the while Juan and
Nita looked on at a safe distance, delighted with
the success of their plan, smiling at each other
as the flames mounted higher and higher.

Burning down a bee-tree proved to be a tedious
process, though, and was not all play. The children had to pack in so much dry wood to keep
the fire up, that they were both quite exhausted.
'Oh, if I only had father's hatchet to cut down
green wood, we could easily do it! This burns
out so fast,' grumbled Juan and then laughed

gleefully, and added, 'Well! I am stupid. Of course I could *cut* it down then and needn't burn it at all.'

While they were talking, crack! crack! went the old tree, and down it fell with a crash! Highly delighted and excited, the children ran up to the edge of the bank, and saw, to their joy, that the tree had split off and open, just as Juan had predicted it would, leaving great flakes and layers of sealed comb in full view. Juan and Nita stood there and gloated over it for a while and then he said, 'Stay here, Nita; I will run back to camp and get one of the deer-hides. It is nicely stretched by this time. Don't touch the comb; the bees will be quiet when I get back, and we can take it all out without any trouble.'

He must have run nearly all the way, he got back so soon with the hide, which he laid down on the ground and quickly covered with fresh leaves. He found the tree even richer than he had expected, and began operations by breaking off some pieces of comb for Nita and himself. These they ate with extreme relish on the bank, and then were very busy and very happy for an hour, putting layer after layer of the delicious stuff into the hide to carry back to camp. The load was a heavy one when they at last started, and they were obliged to stop and rest several times *en route*.

Arrived at their camp they dumped the doe-hide down; and, remembering how much honey had been left behind, made several trips back to the tree, returning with as much comb as they could carry on bark each time. The aggregate was an imposing heap enough; and, well satisfied with themselves and the result of their labors, they stopped only to swing the doe-hide and its contents up on a pliant limb, to get it out of the way of the ants, and lay down on the grass to rest. Their appetites had been considerably blunted by the honey they had eaten; but they managed to dispose of a good deal of venison, all the same.

'By the by, we will get that fawn now,' Juan said, at last. He strung his bow energetically, as he thought of the bag he coveted, and started off, Nita following, while Amigo stopped to finish gnawing at his breakfast of bones.

When they neared the little creature, Nita mustered up her courage and began to plead for its life.

'Don't kill it, Juan, please. I like it. Let me

have it. You can get another. There are plenty
about here. I want it. Do let me keep it, won't
you? If we can't get a shot at another fawn we
can kill this one any time. You can make your
bag of the skin of its little brother that I shot last
night. I want to keep this one, and tame it.
May I not?'

Juan did not at all approve of such a course;
but Nita was so eager and so much in earnest,
that, to please her, he finally put the arrow that
he had chosen for the deed back into the quiver.

'It will die, anyhow,' he said. 'What is the use
of — Well — I will wait.'

Somehow the fawn reminded Nita of her own
feelings when she had been taken from her
mother, and it appealed strongly to her heart.
She had always been fond of pets, too, and had
often wished vainly for a fawn. Dead deer of all
ages were plentiful enough in the Comanche
camp; but here was a living one, and such an
interesting, beautiful little creature, stepping so
daintily, nibbling so prettily, gambolling so playfully! 'No, no! It must not be killed!' she
decided; and, having constituted herself its protector, she thought about it a great deal, and
loved it more and more.

Juan took a good look at the meat he was drying, shifted the pieces about briskly on the poles, made Amigo mount guard over the whole — much against his dogship's will — and then indulged in a short nap.

Nita awoke first, and went in search of her little fawn. It was not far away. Tired out by the wanderings and misfortunes of the last night and day, it was fast asleep when she first caught sight of it, and looked prettier than ever, curled up gracefully among some bushes near the river. She sat down near it, and then and there inaugurated her system of taming wild animals, which, simple as it was, could not have been surpassed by the celebrated Mr. Rarey. The animal before her was neither very wild nor very vicious, it is true; and her method may be broadly said to have consisted in doing nothing at all. Nita was quite half a wild thing herself, and perhaps she knew instinctively how to woo other woodlings, and to teach them to trust her. Certain it is that she waited quietly until the fawn opened its eyes, looked at it quietly, paid no attention to its little snort of fear, watched it bound a few feet away, then slowly crept closer and closer, until, at last, she actually managed to get her hands on the shy creature and give it a caress or two.

After this, she walked back to camp as pleased as possible, and told Juan that he should not touch her little 'Estrella,' as she called the new pet, because it had a white star in the middle of its forehead; fed Amigo; and suggested to Juan that he should drag the carcass of the dead wolf well out of the way, as it was getting offensive. This he did, and, coming back, inspected the four hams hanging up in the tree, gave another turn to the strips on the scaffold, took a look at the hides, and then announced that he was going hunting.

'What's that for, when we have all this?' asked Nita, who was so accustomed to living from hand to mouth that she felt as if they had a wealth of eatables already.

'Oh, I mean to keep the venison for our journey; yes, and kill more and dry it, so it will take up as little space as possible. We won't touch that unless we are forced to,' he replied.

It was getting quite late, so they went off without loss of time to conceal themselves again near the trail by which they had descended into the cañon. This time a flock of turkeys — fine, fat-

looking gobblers, most of them — came down
the trail almost before they got settled, craning
their necks, flying awkwardly over the interven-
ing boulders, squawking noisily the while, coming
in to roost. Nita wanted to let fly at them at
once, but Juan made her wait until they had
drunk all the water they craved and flown up
into the trees. He then crept up cautiously right
under them, and brought down a great big fellow
the first shot. Nita shot, too, almost at the same
moment, but only lost an arrow, as her bird flew
off with it sticking in his body, and the flock
tumbled up and off, and made haste to leave
such a neighborhood. The loss of an arrow was
felt to be a serious one by Nita; they had none
to spare; but she forgot the vexation when Juan
called to her to notice what a fine bird he had
secured.

'It is so fat and heavy that it actually split
open when it fell on its breast,' he said, exultingly.
'We'll take it back to camp, and have the
feathers off in a twinkling. Suppose you do that,
and leave me here to see if I can't get another
shot while you are cooking supper?'

Nita agreed to this, lugged the turkey home,
built a fire, and soon had the long skewer that

she used for roasting (cut and sharpened for her
by Juan) run through the plump breast of a bird
that Apicius would not have scorned. Having
stuck it up before the fire, she sat down to watch
the process, and carefully caught up the juices,
as they poured from the fowl on a large bit of
bark, basted, turned, rebasted, returned, pronounced it 'done,' mentally, wondered why Juan
did not come, got down some honey from the
hive to eat with it, and showed herself a most
thoughtful little housewife. At last, when she
was quite in despair, and her patience all exhausted, she saw Juan coming toward her, and
saw that he was dragging behind him a fawn.
'Can that be my little Estrella?' she thought;
and, forsaking the turkey, ran forward to see,
prepared to be angry and to scold Juan on short
notice. But it was not.

Juan had missed a buck and a doe, but had
killed a fawn, and called out to her:

'You see, I have got another. Come, help me
drag it in. I am tired.'

She obeyed, and they soon had it in camp.
'Now!' she said, and turned toward the spot
where she had left the turkey. It was not there!
She could hardly believe it, she had been gone so

short a time. She looked hastily around, and
caught a glimpse of a bowed head, a guilty
figure, a tail tucked as nearly out of sight as a
tail can be. She understood. It was Amigo who
had done it. The truth was that they had been
so absorbed in their quest of honey, and in har-
vesting the golden stuff, that they had neglected
Amigo a good deal that day. He had not been
fed at the usual hour, and, when he was fed, he
was not given enough to sustain him in a career
of great personal responsibility and unceasing
vigilance; and so he had betrayed his trust, and
anybody could see, even by the flickering fire-
light, that he was deeply ashamed of himself.

Such sincere contrition ought, perhaps, to
have procured his pardon; but he had sinned once
too often. The children were hungry; they had
counted on that turkey; they had not had
turkey since they left the cave, and did not know
when they would get it again. Amigo was
soundly drubbed — 'to teach him a lesson,'
Juan said; but I am afraid there was some anger
and disappointment in the affair. The children
had to sup, after all, on dried venison, and Juan
did not recover from his annoyance until he got
to work butchering the fawn. Nita looked on

with bright interest, Amigo in a broken-hearted, broken-spirited way, while Juan skilfully cut and stripped off the hide so as to make no holes in it, beginning at the neck. The fawn had previously been hung up by its neck so that Juan could get at it easily, and, when he had disposed of the meat, he carried the hide off, sought and found a hole in the rock, put the hide in it, filled it up with ashes and water, and came back to camp again. Nita was extremely curious to see and know what he was about.

'What have you done with it?' she said. 'What do you want with ashes and water? You surely aren't going to pour those on the hide. You will ruin it.'

To this Juan made no reply, except to look very important, and put her off with, 'You will see in due time.'

The first thing Juan did next morning was to have a look at the fawn-skin; and, finding that it had not been in the ashes long enough for the hair to slip off, he determined to leave it where it was, in the tannery he had improvised, overnight.

At breakfast Juanita said to him, 'Don't forget that Amigo has to take his share of our load when we leave here. He can't be a lazy dog when there is so much to carry. You and I won't be able to take it all, and I know he can help.'

'Yes; that was a splendid idea of yours, and I have saved that wolf-skin, and have got it in hand. It will make a splendid pack-saddle,' Juan replied.

He was very impatient to begin the work he had marked out for himself; but it could not be done that day, so he had to content himself with other employments and amusements, of which there was no lack. The most interesting one was shooting two turkeys, which afforded them not only a great deal of fun, but a nice dinner. Anybody could have told that Juan's heart was in the work he had planned, for he was up at dawn next day, and was so full of energy and purpose that he paid no attention to Nita's sleepy remonstrance, 'Don't go yet, Juan; it is not light enough to see.'

'Oh, I can't wait for the sun to get here,' he answered, impatiently, and ran off to the 'tannery.' He soon had the fawn-skin out, shook it thoroughly, and, putting it on a tree that had grown in such a way as to present an inclined plane that exactly served his purpose, he went busily to work. When Nita joined him, he was rubbing away with immense vigor, singing as he bent over the skin, so absorbed in what he was doing that he started when she spoke to him. She offered to help, and looked on with vivid curiosity, as Juan swept up and down the skin with a deer-rib, and skilfully removed the hair. She chattered to him all the while, and plied him with questions; but he only continued to sing and to work.

'Now, then,' he said at last, when the skin was all clean and smooth, 'you can run back to camp, and bring me all the turkey-fat there is. Hurry up!'

Full of admiration of Juan's talent and ingenuity, Nita cheerfully obeyed; and, as a reward, was allowed to take a turn at rubbing the fat into the skin when Juan's arms and muscles gave out. When it was thoroughly soaked with fat, and had been rubbed until it seemed a wonder that there was anything left of it, they took it up between them and bore it proudly back to camp, and propped it up in front of the fire to dry. They then breakfasted on cold turkey, and, as they munched away, discussed their plans.

'As soon as I have done, I shall begin Amigo's

pack-saddle; for we shall have to accustom him gradually to wearing it. Don't you interfere, Nita. I'll bring him to terms,' said Juan. 'You can just amuse yourself with your fawn. How tame it is already! It joins the deer that come in to water every night. I wonder it hasn't gone off with them. What was the use of taking it for a pet, anyhow? We shall not be here longer than a week, and then you will have to leave it.'

'But I won't leave it! I am not going to leave my little Estrella behind me,' replied Nita pettishly. 'I like it better than any pet I ever had, and I mean to take it with me.'

'All right; only I will kill it first,' said Juan teasingly.

'You shan't kill it, at all,' said Nita; 'it is mine. I won't have it killed. And we are not going away in a week; we are going to stay a month. You said so yourself.'

'Oh, that was when I first came, and I was tired! I am going just as soon as I am ready,' said Juan.

'But I am not going until I am ready,' retorted Nita.

'You are going whenever I see fit to take you,' said Juan provokingly. 'I am a warrior, and I

know best, and you must do as I say. You are
nothing but a child, and you will never be anything but a squaw. We are going in a week, and
I shall kill your fawn whenever I choose.'

Then followed a stormy moment, full of 'I
shalls' and 'I shan'ts,' 'I wills' and 'I won'ts,'
which worked the quarrel up to its height. Never
had they had such a disagreement, and their
hearts were so full of angry and wicked feelings
that even the lovely Cañon of Roses became all
at once an ugly and dreadful place.

'I will kill it now,' said Juan passionately,
starting up and seizing his bow.

'You shan't touch it!' shrieked Nita.

Both children ran as fast as they could to
where Estrella was peacefully grazing, in ignorance of what was going on. Quick as thought,
Nita rushed up to it. Quicker still, Juan fitted
an arrow and let it drive. But not into the fawn
did it go. Nita had thrown her arms around her
little pet's neck, and whiz went the arrow into
the fleshy part of her left arm! She gave a shriek,
and tumbled down as if killed.

Juan was dreadfully frightened. His anger
cooled at once, and was replaced by alarm and
regret. He ran forward, startling the fawn,

which bounded away a short distance, and looked back at the children, quite unconscious of its narrow escape. Juan passionately assured Nita that he had not meant to hurt her; he whipped out his knife, cut off the point of the arrow, sacrificing it without a thought, drew it out with one swift motion, and, in a twinkling, had stanched the blood that flowed from the wound, and bound up her arm with more skill and gentleness than could have been expected. So eager was he, so humble, so penitent, that Nita could not long remain estranged and unforgiving.

Realizing, as they did, that they both had been in fault, no sooner did one begin to take all the blame for what had happened, than the other, too, assumed it; and never had their hearts been more closely united than when they finally embraced each other, after half an hour of sighs and tears, excuses, explanations, and confessions.

Juan's generous nature was especially moved, and he ardently longed to make every possible reparation. He could not sufficiently accuse himself, and, as to Estrella, he conceded everything. He would catch and tame several fawns for her, if she liked; he would do anything, agree to anything, that would make Nita happy.

Meanwhile, the innocent cause of the well-nigh tragic dispute had wandered off a little way, and seemed to be looking at them in mild rebuke.

The truth was that Juan had been growing more and more proud and overbearing of late. He had convinced himself that he was a very remarkable boy; indeed, infinitely superior, not only to Nita, but to everybody; and this conviction had led him to treat his sister with a certain contempt which she had felt, but had not resented. He saw his mistake now; and, as they walked back to camp, he was so kind and tender, so humble, and so like his old self, that Nita's love and confidence revived tenfold.

Nor was this the only good result that flowed from the quarrel. The remembrance of the lengths to which his anger had carried him kept him on his guard against giving way to his temper, and taught him to curb his passionate nature. As for Nita, she asked nothing better than to live in love and peace with Juan.

In this way another member was added to the party in the cañon, and, for the remainder of their stay, Estrella was as much at home in the camp as Amigo. There was never a prettier or gentler little creature. It became wonderfully

tame, and would follow Nita about as if it had
been a pet lamb — up the valley, down the
valley, across the river — wherever that active
young mistress chose to rove; it would eat from
her hand and rub against her, cat-fashion; it
seemed to her to have every delightful quality
that a pet could have, and she was never tired of
caressing it. It is certain that she never would
have given it up of her own accord; and Juan was
not only pledged to non-interference, but hardly
dared reopen the subject lest he and Nita should
quarrel again and make each other miserable.

Estrella finally settled it once for all. She took
her future into her own hands, or rather hoofs;
and one night, when the children were fast asleep,
and the crescent moon was peering over the edge
of the cliff, with one horn well down to see if those
could possibly be the two little Mexicans that
had escaped from the Comanches, the little fawn
trotted off down the river-bank, plashed into the
water and joined a certain benevolent doe that
frequented the cañon. We have nothing to do
with the interview between them. It was not
their first; and Estrella's comical little tail
wagged a great deal while it lasted, perhaps from
satisfaction at finding herself an adopted child.

IT BECAME WONDERFULLY TAME, AND WOULD FOLLOW NITA ABOUT
AS IF IT HAD BEEN A PET LAMB

An hour later she might have been seen leaping up a well-known trail in the wake of her foster-mother and beautiful young foster-brother.

The party took their way to the plateau above, and so on out into the hills, where, all unmindful of the affection, sacrifices, and distress of the mistress she had abandoned, the happy, if ungrateful, fawn went back to that state of nature which for her and all her tribe is emphatically a state of grace as well.

CHAPTER IX

SEÑOR LEOPARDO

NITA's wound made her feverish that night, and Juan could not sleep for thinking of her and of what he had done. He rose several times, and insisted on bathing her arm freely with cold water; he made her a bed of fragrant grasses, piled high around her; he awoke her more than once, to ask anxiously how she felt. 'This is the way in which I have kept my promise to the mother, always to take care of Juanita,' he thought, in bitter self-reproach. He made himself very unhappy lest the wound should not heal well, and further trouble be in store for him, and could hardly wait for the light to come to run off into the nearest wood in search of certain leaves which the Comanches use for medicinal purposes.

When Nita opened her eyes, Juan was not to be seen; but in about an hour he came running swiftly toward camp, holding out his olive-branch, the leaves he had been in search of, and had only found up on the plateau, five miles away. Of these he made a kind of poultice with water, bruising them first between two flat stones, and bound it on her arm, an expedition and surgical operation which he insisted on repeating every day for a week. His affectionate care made Nita so happy that it seemed to her almost worth while to be shot in order to be so kindly nursed; and, being accustomed to see the gravest illness and most severe hurts silently endured, she made no sort of lamentation or complaint. She insisted that her wound was nothing, and would have occupied herself very much as usual, had she not seen that it worried Juan to have her use her arm. As it was, she kept quiet, and this, with Juan's poultice, so aided the natural process by which nature repairs the wrongs done a healthy body, that a complete cure was soon effected, to her comfort and Juan's great joy.

Meanwhile, she had to sit and look on while her brother busied himself in making two things in which they were both deeply interested — a pack-saddle and saddle-bags for Amigo. With his usual cleverness and ingenuity, Juan, in three days, deftly fashioned the first out of the wolf-skin he had saved and tanned. In three more he made a serviceable, if not particularly handsome pair of bags out of the doe-hide. And then came the necessity of trying both on the person for whom they were intended, and reconciling him to their use.

Now, it must be quite clear by this time that Amigo was an uncommonly sagacious and right-minded dog — a dog of fine intelligence, good principle (as canine principles go), and warm heart; but still he was a dog. He had no objection whatever to making himself useful, and knew very well that he had the brains and ability to serve his master. Could he not, when he lived at the *hacienda*, go out into the open prairie and pick out from fifty herds every horse, cow, calf, and sheep belonging to Don José, and drive them into the *corral*, and that alone, and at the same hour every evening? Had he not looked after the cattle for three years because he was told to do so, although he would have greatly preferred to be about his proper business, which was herding sheep?

It was, then, not from any stupidity or desire to shirk unpleasant duties that Amigo proved to be a difficult subject for training as a beast of burden. It was only, as I have already said, that he was a dog. When everything was ready, Juan whistled to him, and he came running out of the bushes readily enough, and came up to where they were sitting, Juan with the pack-saddle in his hand eager to adjust it, Nita longing to have a share in the transaction, and deeply interested to see how it would succeed.

Both children began talking to Amigo, exactly as though he had been a human being; and no human being could have looked more intelligent than he did as he stood there listening, wagging his tail, smiling in their faces while they explained the necessity they were under of exacting from him a service he had never rendered before. He stood perfectly still while Juan put the saddle on, and both children were so delighted by his docility and appearance that they capered about him in high glee, laughing heartily to see their old friend in such a queer new rôle, and charmed with the entire success of Nita's plan for securing a porter.

However, they congratulated themselves prematurely; for, growing tired of standing still and being admired, Amigo suddenly sat down, when lo! off slipped the saddle, and, thinking the children's little game at an end, Amigo bounded off up the river-bank again. He was called back, and Juan set to work to remedy the fault. It was not so easy for an amateur saddler to manage this, though, and Juan spent an hour trying to contrive a set of harness that would serve his purpose. Tie as he would, and strap as he would, the saddle would slip down when Amigo sat down, as sit he would, or be shaken off, perhaps, for Amigo soon got to think the whole thing a nuisance, and was minded to get out of it if he could.

Finally, by an ingenious system of breast and tail straps, Juan got the saddle arranged in such a way that, run and rub and wriggle as Amigo might, he could not get it off, and then he cut some fresh thongs of leather, and bound the saddle-bags into place. Amigo was then much patted and praised, and half coaxed, half forced, to trot down the valley for about half a mile and back again, when he was released and given a large piece of turkey, as a reward for what, on the whole, was good behavior.

This was the first lesson, and it was repeated every day, the load which was to be carried being gradually added, and the distance increased. For a few days either Juan or Nita always ran alongside, and kept fast hold of a leather strap fastened around Amigo's neck; but, seeing that the dog was beginning to understand what was required of him, Juan took off the strap, and, by dint of giving Amigo a blow or two when he ran into the undergrowth, and some very nice bones when he trotted along soberly and properly by his master — in short, by a judicious system of rewards and punishments — soon converted the sensible shepherd-dog into an excellent pack-animal.

As may be supposed, the children thoroughly enjoyed training him, and spent many an hour in the merriest fashion running after or before him, heading him off in this direction, driving him in that. To saddle and unsaddle him, alone, was an amusement of which they never tired, and Amigo made less and less resistance to the process; indeed, soon gave himself the air of having been in the business all his life.

At last a day came when the children had no longer an excuse for staying any longer in the cañon, and began to think of moving on. They were no longer weary or footsore; they had as much dried meat as they could possibly carry; and there was no reason why they should not start at once. Yet, with a not unnatural horror of what might lie before them, they talked of going for several days before they could make up their minds to leave their beautiful cañon, offering them, as it did, shelter, food, water, shade, and an endless variety of pleasures.

'Let us stay just this day, and play in the river,' said Nita; or, 'I must climb up the cliff, and get some more roses to make a necklace for Estrella.'

'I should like another shot from the upper trail; we may as well kill one more turkey, and stay another day,' said Juan.

Nita was more willing to go, after Estrella took French leave of them in that very garland of roses, and Juan felt that he ought not to waste any more time; so it was decided one night, when all the cañon was dimly suffused with moonlight, and a mocking-bird close by was pouring out a perfect rainbow of song over the heads of the children, who were lying under the tree in which a certain nest had been made.

'It is a paradise,' said Juan for the twentieth time; 'but we must leave it.'

The paradise he had in mind was the Indian one, which consists of a lovely spot where there are plenty of enormous acorns for bread, luxuriant clover as pasture for horses, an abundance of fat venison, cold, sparkling water, and grass that never fails; but the term might have been carelessly applied to the cañon at that moment by the most orthodox Christian.

'Casteel will be a grizzly bear, that is certain,' said Nita, whose mind often reverted to that terrible warrior. She had always been told in the tribe that bad Indians, when they died, either became grizzly bears, or wandered forever in a sterile land, where game was scarce and wild, acorns small, and water brackish, and she had privately settled that the last fate was not the one reserved for Casteel. She knew that if there was any game at all in that country Casteel would contrive to kill it, and make himself comfortable somehow; and her imagination had long fed upon the image of Casteel as a savage, wicked, hungry, helpless bear, powerless to help himself or hurt others. The poor child's religious impressions were the strangest possible jumble of Comanche and Catholic ideas by this time; and the mere thought of her old enemy in that alarming guise frightened her so that she crossed herself and said, 'Don't let us talk of Casteel any more, Juan, dear.'

'I am not talking of him, or thinking of him,' replied Juan. 'I am thinking that we must leave this before daylight to-morrow. We will take advantage of these fine nights to travel only partly by day; and, now that we have so much food, and can carry so much water, I don't believe we shall suffer as we have done.'

After this there was a long pause. Juan was revolving the journey in his mind, and thinking out his plans. Nita had no such responsibility, and had almost dropped asleep, when she was roused by an energetic shake from Juan.

'Nita, Nita, I have been thinking. I have got such an idea! Body of San Hippolito![1] why didn't I think of it when I saw those Lipans starting off, and follow in their wake? But no! that would not have done either. They would have made all the game so wild that we should have starved.'

'Heavens above, *hermano mio!* what are you talking about?' inquired Nita, surprised and confused by all these allusions. 'Follow the Lipans, indeed! You must be crazy! What do you mean?'

'Mean? Why, don't you see? They did not go

[1] Hippolito is patron of lunatics and idiots.

toward Mexico; and I saw them set their faces toward Texas, and never thought why. Oh, it is too much, such stupidity!' exclaimed Juan, with vehemence.

'Well, what if they did? I am sure I didn't want to follow them, or have them follow us,' said Nita, with entire sincerity.

'But don't you see?' persisted Juan. '*They struck for the nearest point* — the nearest settlement. Texas, then, must be much nearer us than Mexico; and if they can go there, we can go, too. I can't imagine what made me such a dolt as not to see it before. I shall change our course, and make for Texas. There are Mexicans there, I have heard, and we can easily get from there to Mexico in some way. *Viva!* Nita! It is a splendid thought. It is as clear as daylight to me now.'

It was not quite so easy for Nita to change her views about the route to be taken, and she argued the question for some little time with Juan; but of course yielded in the end, after which they both went contentedly to sleep.

The morning star was still shining in the first auroral flush of coming day, when Juan and Nita once more stood together on the plateau above

the cañon, which they had left in darkness.
They had crossed the river, and walked down
three miles to another opening, which they had
previously explored, and knew would take them
out on the prairie beyond. The sound of falling
water (coming from the river running over a
series of rocky ledges, and finally leaping into a
pool below near the deer-run they were mount-
ing) reached them for some time, as did the odor
of the roses, which grew as luxuriantly about
there as they did near their abandoned camp;
and when they finally reached the plateau, and
saw the great, wide plain stretching away before
them, Nita's first impulse was to beg Juan to go
back to the cañon.

It seemed a dreadful thing to start out into
that dark, unknown country. But he was not one
whit dismayed, and broke into a whistle, which
he presently cut short to say, 'A good, early
start this, Nita. We turn southward now, and
we ought to get a long march done and over before noon. What are you doing?'

Nita, yielding to a natural impulse, was peering over the side of the precipice. Juan joined
her, and also looked down into the mysterious
abyss.

'Don't you think we — we had better go back?' suggested Nita timidly.

'No!' replied Juan with much emphasis; and, impatient to be off, he marched away at once across the prairie, with Amigo bounding along at his heels.

As the light grew brighter Nita's heart grew lighter, and the brother and sister were soon walking with more spirit, and talking with more cheerfulness, than they had done since they started. For one thing, they felt secure from the two great dangers that had so long threatened them, starvation and thirst; for another, hope of reaching the settlements sooner than they had at first thought possible, had inspired them with astonishing energy.

'I think that the worst is over for us,' said Juan. 'With Amigo's help we can carry enough water and provisions to last for ten days at a time; and in that time we can certainly replenish our store, unless we are very unfortunate.'

In this faith the party travelled for an entire week without other stoppages than such as were necessary, and absolutely without adventures of any kind. And Juan was right; the worst was over. Fatigues and hardships up to a certain point were to be their portion for many weeks to come; but want and misery were at an end, as we shall see. The first they bore with that stolidity which was partly habit, partly training; the second they were happily not called upon to endure again.

In a few days the character of the scenery about them began to change for the better, and they soon entered a lovely country, richly wooded, looking for all the world with its short turf and fine oaks, its glades and dells, and its exquisite undulations, like an English park. With its distant line of blue mountains, its herds of deer, its beautiful streams and carpet of wildflowers, there was nothing that the most accomplished landscape-gardener could have added to heighten the charming effect; and for once art and nature were interchangeable terms. They had left the high tablelands behind them, and entered the delightful region adjoining. They noticed that the evening star no longer cast a shadow. The heat was still very great, but had lost its peculiar oppressive quality, and there were no more bare, shelterless prairies to traverse — arid wastes oppressive to the imagination, stretching away in desolate monotony to the very skyline. They had but crossed a small portion of one such, that ended four hundred miles away in the deserts of Arizona.

Every day carried them farther into this beautiful district; and, although they only looked at it from the practical and personal standpoint of its capacity to sustain three travellers cast upon its tender mercies, yet, even so, it was all that was cheering, and insensibly they were much affected by its charming aspect. For some time they were very independent, and made no demands upon it, pushing steadily on, with no thought of anything except getting over as much ground as possible. The fine, pure air of that region made these long marches less trying than more moderate exertion taken in a different climate, and the children took a pride in taxing their endurance to its utmost limit, feeling that every mile was just that much gained, and brought them that much nearer the *hacienda*.

They were quite free from care for the present; but Juan was not sorry to see that the country was full of game, from buffalo to rabbits. The sight of it excited Amigo very much, and at first he was for chasing every rabbit and fowl that crossed his path; but he soon learned that he must control himself, and not give way to such impulses. It was wonderful to see how well and faithfully he bore his burdens and played his part. Occasionally he would get wedged in between the bushes in a way to threaten the cargo he carried, and would have to be disentangled by one of the children, and he had a trick of lying down when he got hot and tired, and required a good deal of coaxing and encouragement sometimes to induce him to resume the march. But, on the whole, he behaved astonishingly well, and trotted many a mile behind his young master and mistress in the most sober and responsible fashion. His eyes rolled longingly to the right or left; his tongue lolled out of his mouth with heat and fatigue; that odious saddle rubbed and chafed his poor back not a little, and he was often dead tired and covered with perspiration; but he kept straight on in the path of duty, which was the more creditable, in that he knew no reason for hurrying through such a pleasant country.

On the ninth day out, the children came upon a beautiful valley and had hardly traversed three miles of it when what should they see but a river curving boldly into it and running away in a southeasterly direction. Now they could see its long bend sparkling in the sunshine, and at the next turn it would be concealed by its own wooded banks; but there it was. There was water, shade, rest, all manner of delightful things, and they pressed on toward it with the utmost eagerness. When they got up to it Amigo's sorely tried principles gave way under the strain of a new and overpowering temptation. He dashed off toward the stream, and in another moment would have been in it had not Juan rushed after him and caught him just in time.

'Poor old fellow! does he want a bath? Well, wait a minute, just one minute, until I get off this saddle,' said Juan, and fell to untying and unbuckling a dozen or so of straps.

The moment he was free, Amigo gave a tremendous bound and rush, and the next instant had plunged into the water, and was swimming downstream in a state of evident ecstasy that amused the children immensely. It was not very long before they were indulging in the same luxury, and a luxury it was, after their long journey. They spent an hour most agreeably in swimming and shouting, and laughing, and floating, and ducking, and diving, and every imaginable antic; and Amigo took a lively part in

their play, fetched sticks, no matter where Juan
threw them, swam up and down and all around
and looked delightfully absurd with the water
dripping off his nose and tail, and his honest
countenance radiating satisfaction.

When they were all on dry land again, Juan
called to Nita to come lower down and look at
the quantities of fish that were now to be seen in
the stream they had quitted; great trout swimming lazily along, schools of perch swimming
swiftly on their own errands, blue catfish darting
here and there. Nita took a good look at them
all, and heartily echoed Juan's 'It is too bad, a
river full of fish, and no way in the world of
catching them.' They returned the compliment,
and some instinct seemed to tell them that their
natural enemy was at hand, for they ran away
under the banks and rocks in a great panic, and
soon there was not a fish to be seen except the
phlegmatic cat, which, quite unaffected by all
this commotion, moved about tranquilly, deep
down in the clear water. As their fright wore off,
they all came back again, curious to see the
dreadful new creatures that had so startled them;
and the sight made Juan sigh afresh. He was especially fond of fish, and he felt the loss of his

tackle to be more of a grievance than ever. 'If I only had a little horsehair, I know what I would do,' he said. 'What a supper we would have! I would shoot those trout if we had any arrows to spare; but we haven't, and I don't like to risk losing them. And you know when an arrow gets wet it is generally useless. The sinew that is used to fasten on the feathers and spike becomes soft and comes off, and the arrow will warp. Well, I suppose I must give up all idea of fish for supper; but I'll get something, and you had better fill the canteens and make a fire, Nita. Fortunately there can be no lack of food here.' So saying, he gave a last lingering look at the biggest trout in sight, and walked away back to the spot where they had left the pack.

The shadows were now lengthening, but were far from bringing peace and quiet to the place. The children found it full of stir and motion. Turkeys were coming in, all gobble and yelp, to roost for the night; squirrels were chattering overhead; covies of quail flew up under their very feet, and nearly made Amigo jump out of his skin; whole flocks of ducks went squawking and quacking past them; and suddenly three successive white clouds of pigeons swept past them, flying so near the ground that Nita was forced to dodge her head left, right, left again to avoid being struck. They were probably on their way to their roosting-places, hundreds of miles away, and were naturally in a hurry, for at best they can't get much sleep. They keep late hours, come in long after dark, and then take so long to settle down for the night, with all their fluttering, crowding, changes and confusion (to say nothing of breaking a limb or two by persisting in all flocking upon that one and no other), that it must be nearly daylight before they can close an eye.

Juan caught sight of some deer feeding in the distance, but concluded to sup on turkey. Before the sun dropped quite out of sight behind the distant mountains, he had two on spits before the fire; and, after the dry fare of the last week, our travellers greatly relished the breast of these delicious birds. They had a merry little meal together, and did not stint themselves at all, seeing that it would hardly require any exertion to get food enough for a whole tribe, much less for three runaways. Amigo, overjoyed at being relieved from his pack-saddle, frisked about extensively, and went off at short intervals on voyages of discovery all that evening, but finally

settled down at their feet when the children lay
down under a large pecan tree.

The night was not only fine and clear, but
moonlit and wonderfully brilliant. In that lati-
tude, and at that altitude, moonlight means a
good deal more than the feeble, glimmering light
that gives such an effect of mournfulness and
desolation to even the most prosperous land-
scapes in northern countries. This was not a
tearful, unhappy moon in reduced circumstances, but the beautiful queen of the night,
shining afar in splendid state, and flooding the
world with a light as clear, if incomparably softer
than that of her rival the sun. The wind from
the river was balmy and delightful; the place
was full of sweet repose, and absolutely peaceful.
The children were tired young things, and were
soon lulled to sleep, their last feeling one of perfect comfort and security.

How long Juan slept he never knew; he was to
all intents and purposes a Comanche, and an
Indian never seems to sleep at all in the sense of
losing all consciousness of what is happening
around him; so perhaps it is not remarkable that
Juan, whose ear was next the ground, suddenly
opened his eyes, then sat up, then laid his ear

down to the earth again, and again sat up and looked eagerly about him. He had heard a sound that he very well knew, and he was awaiting further developments. He had to wait a good while first, and in the interval he awoke Nita gently, and told her in a whisper that he had heard the sound of horses' feet, and then placed himself so that he could clap his hand over Amigo's mouth and smother a bark if need be.

'Oh, Juan! it's Indians. It is the Comanches,' whispered Nita, in abject fright.

'Comanches! Nonsense! There isn't a Comanche within a hundred miles,' he replied.

'Then it is the Apaches,' said Nita, fastening upon another tribe, also the terror of the border settlements. 'Oh, do let us run and hide somewhere! Don't stay here, Juan.'

'Run, indeed! I am surprised at you, Nita. Never run as long as you are not seen, or can hide. S — sh! not another word.'

With this, Juan proceeded to practise the silence he had enjoined, and Nita could hear nothing but the rustling leaves about her. There was a long silence, and then Nita heard, first very faintly, and then quite distinctly, the sound of which Juan had spoken. Her heart beat with the utmost violence as it grew louder and clearer; but she did not disobey Juan or shriek or cry. She just edged up as close to her brother as she could, and caught hold of his arm.

In another moment they saw something that they never afterwards forgot. The boughs at a little distance on the right parted, and a herd of wild horses came trotting along under the wide-spreading boughs of the fine oaks and cotton-woods of the grove. The leader of the band, a beautiful white stallion, with long, flowing mane and tail, came first, and was not far from them when Amigo, as Juan had foreseen, gave a bark, or rather attempted to give one. Juan's hand was so promptly applied that only a stifled snort escaped; but, slight as the noise was, it reached the leader, who wheeled and ran back a short distance, the herd doing the same. The children were in deep shadow, and could see them perfectly, especially the leader. The beautiful creature stood there for several minutes, his flanks flecked with the flickering shadows of the leaves overhead, his head full in the moonlight, his whole attitude one of the most exquisite freedom and grace, his large eyes making a circuit of the wood about him with anxious intentness.

Hearing nothing but the night wind, and seeing
nothing to further alarm him, he evidently concluded that he had been mistaken in supposing
that there was any danger; and, with a bold toss
of his mane, he bounded forward again with a
light, swift movement, indescribably charming,
and plunged into the river. He was followed by
the whole herd, of course.

Juan and Nita caught a glimpse of a fine,
black stallion, and some mares and colts. They
heard the splash, splash of water, and were about
to get up and go down to the river to get another
look at the beautiful wild creatures that had so
fascinated them, when suddenly a sound as of
breaking boughs reached them, and then a
terrific scream of mingled fright and pain, unlike
anything they had ever known or imagined — a
shriek human in its agony, and demoniacal in its
tone — rent the quiet night. Poor Nita fell back
against the nearest tree in almost mortal terror,
and Juan sprang to his feet, whistled for Amigo
and dashed off in the direction of the river.
Afraid to be left alone, Nita rushed after him
with all her speed.

While they had been quietly sleeping in the
shadow of that pecan tree, a leopard had been in

hiding in a dwarf-oak, not fifty feet away, waiting
for the herd of mustangs to come in to water. As
the last colt passed him, he sprang upon its back,
drove his cruel claws deep into its back, and
began savagely tearing off great strips of flesh.
Maddened at finding himself ridden by such a
master, the poor colt galloped frantically out of
the wood, and up the bank of the river, plunged
into the water, felt those terrible claws only
sinking the deeper, turned back to the bank
again, reared, plunged, snorted, bounded into
the wood, and tried to rub the leopard off against
the trees, rushed out on the bank again, gave
vent to screams so terrible that Juanita's hair
almost stood on end, and finally dropped down
and rolled over in a death agony, not five hundred yards from where the children were standing.

The herd knew very well what had happened,
and scattered in every direction. The mother of
the colt and the leader of the band, on hearing
the first shriek, wheeled about in the river, and
ran back toward the leopard; but, as soon as they
got a whiff of him, and heard his growl, they
swerved aside, and galloped after the herd with
all their might, the leader looking more beautiful

than ever, his wet white coat glittering in the moonlight, his long white tail held out almost at right angles from his body, his very mane stiff with fright, as he raced up the bank, and disappeared in the woods.

The incomparable speed, grace, and beauty of the lovely, free creature riveted Juan's eyes as long as he was in sight, and it was with throbbing pulses and a beating heart that he turned to see what had become of the leopard. The children were on the edge of the wood, and were concealed from view, but could plainly see all that was happening on the bank — too plainly, Nita thought, as, with chattering teeth and dilated eyes, she followed the movements of the various animals. Some dark, moving objects were still to be seen in the silvery stream spread out before them, the horses that had taken that way of escape, but all their attention was now claimed by the leopard, who, having killed the colt, was dragging it off, quite unconscious of being observed, luckily for the observers. Like the African animal of the same species he was a large, powerful, beautiful beast. His yellow hide glowed golden in that mellow light, and was dotted with jet-black spots. If pinched by hunger, he would not have hesitated to attack a man, even, much less two children. With majestic evil grace he carried the colt a short distance, and, having eaten his fill, walked all around it, as if to regard it from every point of view, and then carefully covered the carcass with leaves, and walked slowly away toward his den, which was on the other side of the river in a cliff of rock.

If the children had watched this performance with the utmost intentness, Amigo had devoured it, but for a different reason. He bristled up, and would have growled and barked more than once but for Juan's vigorous measures. It was all very well for that leopard to kill a colt, but Amigo thought he knew who ought to eat it, and he chafed very much at the restraint laid upon him. For some time after the leopard was out of sight, Juan kept perfectly still, and laid his finger on his lip, fearing that the leopard might come back again to look after its prey; but at last he left the shelter of the tree that had screened them, and began to talk freely to Nita of what they had seen.

Great was her astonishment to find that he had positively enjoyed a scene that had terrified her half to death. He was full of satisfaction at having seen a leopard for the first time.

'They are very scarce, you know, and getting scarcer every year, Casteel says. Wasn't it a beauty! How I would like to tackle it, if I were a man! And that white horse! Oh, if I could only catch him, and tame him! What a war-horse he would make!' he said. And when Nita had confided, in turn, all that she had feared and suffered, she begged him to leave that dreadful place without a moment's loss of time. 'It is rather a dangerous neighborhood, and we had better get away from it,' he agreed, 'but I am going to steal a meal or two from Señor Leopardo first.'

This proposition did not strike Nita as it would have done an American child; for she was accustomed to eating horse-flesh; and, like the Comanches, thought a young mule the best of all meats. So she looked on with much sympathy and no disgust, while Juan uncovered the colt, pulled a great bunch of hair from his tail, and adroitly cut off several steaks for their use, and a huge slice for Amigo, who disposed of his share then and there. Feeling uneasy about the leopard, they only waited after this to get their packs, and saddle Amigo, when they started off down the river, nor did they stop until they had put a good ten miles between themselves and a terrible enemy.

CHAPTER X

SOME GOOD SPORT AND A FRESH PERIL

HAVING secured, thus unexpectedly, the horse-hair he had coveted, Juan promptly proceeded to make use of it, and was no sooner awake the next morning than he fell to twisting the hair into a strong line, which he then fixed to a bone hook such as I have already described. He was determined to have fish for breakfast; and, with a small piece of the mustang for bait, was soon angling successfully; and he had six large perch broiling on the coals before he called Nita, who, tired out with the excitement of the previous night and a long walk, was still sound asleep. This comfortably disposed of, they resumed their journey until noon, when they stopped, and cooked the last of their meat, which they thought as nice as possible.

'We are well out of that leopard's way, now,' replied Juan, at dinner, 'and we may as well rest awhile here and do a little hunting. What do you say to quail for supper, Nita?'

Nita was pleased enough by the prospect of trapping quail; and she and Juan had no sooner finished their meal than they set to work to make the necessary preparations for that very favorite sport. They first made some stout loops of horse-hair, and fastened them to wooden pegs which they drove into the ground under the bushes where they saw the quail were in the habit of congregating. Nita then scattered some seed and berries about; and, having done all they could to lure the birds to destruction, they further deter-mined to try another plan. They cut a long, slender pole apiece, put a horsehair noose on the end, and, with this simple contrivance, started out to catch quail in a fashion that is quite com-mon in western Texas. Amigo followed them, which was just as well, since they could not have accomplished anything without his assist-ance.

They had not gone far before they saw a large covey of quail run and hide behind some thick bushes. Going as near as they could without startling the birds into flight, Juan and Nita waited a moment, and then charged them with loud yells and set Amigo on them. As eager for good sport as either Juan or Nita he ran right into the covey. The quail flew up and lit all around in the trees, where they sat in a curious state of immobility, as if petrified by fright. Juan and Nita kept up a tremendous din all the while in order that this desirable effect might not wear off; and, walking under the motionless birds, managed, with infinite dexterity, to slip the noose of horsehair over the head of first one and then another fowl, each time giving their poles a quick jerk that brought the bird in the bush well in hand, fluttering down on the end of the pole, indeed, apparently paralyzed by the audacity of the hunters.

They kept this up until they had secured all the birds that had lit low enough to be reached, and then went on until they came upon another covey, which they served in exactly the same way. After an hour of capital sport and fun, they returned to camp with no less than twenty nice fat birds, which they proceeded to pick and clean. It was too soon to think of supping, so they hung the birds around on the bushes near their camp-fire (which gave their temporary resting-place a great look of comfort and plenty), and gave the rest of the afternoon to looking for honey to eat with the quail. This was a very hard matter, and the quest was one that the children, with their childish taste for sweet things, always especially enjoyed. Hives so abound in that region that the swarms of bees that have left the old home will sometimes commence work wherever they first settle; though, as a rule, they exhibit a decided talent for selecting inaccessible spots, as hard to rob as a cliff-swallow's nest.

This time the children had the luck to come upon a hive which was within easy reach; and, having eaten all they wanted, they carried back a nice supply to camp. On the way they killed three squirrels, and were engaged in skinning them in front of the fire, when they heard a flopping of wings, and an old turkey flew up off the ground and lit in the oak above their very heads. From this elevated perch he began craning his neck down to get a good look at the strangers who had presumed to invade his hereditary roosting-place, and cried out 'Put! put!' which in the turkey tongue means 'Go away immediately.' Instead of taking the hint, however, both Juan and Nita sent an arrow into his side at a given signal, and down he tumbled, almost in the fire, creating a great commotion. Amigo, who had, in an eminent degree, that attribute of genius which consists in seizing an opportunity and making the most of it, got several mouthfuls of feathers out of him before Juan could interfere, or the turkey could flutter out of the way.

Here, then, were work and food in abundance, and it was quite dark by the time the children had finished picking their remarkably fat old gobbler, and had cleaned and spitted him, and hung him up near the other birds, where he had, at least, the advantage of plenty of good company. They ran off, and picked up some dead live-oak limbs which they heaped on the fire, and sat up quite late that night, cooking, and eating, and talking.

Finding that Nita was afraid to go to sleep, for fear of wild animals in general, and leopards in particular, Juan collected a quantity of brush, and together they made a little house of the thorny bushes, into which they crept, and then pulled more brush in, so as to completely close up the aperture. Their 'lodge,' as Juan called it, fairly bristled with thorns, and would have effectually defended them from almost any enemy; but none came prowling about. Nita lay awake for a long while, listening for stealthy footsteps and strange sounds. She could not get out of her mind the image of the poor colt and its terrible rider. The piercing shrieks of the wretched animal still rang in her ears, and she still saw its frantic agony; that mad rush up and down the river-bank in the moonlight; the blood that streamed down its back and flanks from the wicked claws buried deep in the quivering flesh; the expression of the leopard as he sat there in savage mastery, the very embodiment of cruel power — every feature of the diabolical triumph was repeated again and again in the child's dreams, and three times she awoke Juan by her labored groans and cries.

She was not sorry, when morning came, to push aside the rude door of the lodge, and find herself in the world of realities again. The fire had burned down into a fine bed of coals; and, turning with relief from the horrors of the past night, to the duties of the present, Nita soon had seven quail broiling most satisfactorily, in preparation for breakfast, and had filled the canteens, and brought in four fagots of wood before Juan came yawning out of doors. When they had broken their fast, they cooked the remainder of their birds, Nita giving especial attention to the roasting of the gobbler, on which they meant to dine.

As Nita watched the streams of gravy that ran

down the stick on which it was spitted she could not help exclaiming, 'Oh, if we only had some of our mother's *tortillas* to eat with it!' She had made the remark at least fifty times before; but, if not novel, it was appropriate, and Juan not only echoed the wish, as usual, but added, 'We shall have some of them soon, *hermanita mia*. We have travelled a great distance already; and, if we keep on, we shall strike the Texan frontier somewhere in a few weeks. Oh, what joy to see our mother!' ('*Madre preciosa*,' was the phrase Juan used) — and thus introduced the topic of which they never tired — *home*.

The conversation lasted an hour, and they settled a great many things in the course of it. What they would say and do on their arrival; what the Señora would not only say and do, but think; how old Santiago and the herders would be astonished by what they had to tell; how Padre Garcia would be sure to weep, for he was always crying anyway, and would then give them his blessing; how Amigo would be lionized, and how everybody would try to buy him, quite in vain; how they would herd the cattle and sheep as their father had done, only much better, and show the Mexican children a thing or two about shooting with a bow, and hunting. They even settled that they would get home before the Señora was out of bed in the morning, and rush in and throw themselves upon her without any warning. It was delightful talk to them, and they kept it up until it was time to saddle Amigo and be off.

The river, happily, was running in the direction Juan desired to take; so they kept along its banks, but at a respectful distance, for they found that Amigo was a very refractory horse when they were near the water, and would keep on trotting off at a tangent, making for the river, and threatening the loss of his cargo, if not of his pack. They kept in sight of the stream, and went down to it whenever they got hot or thirsty, usually at meal-time only, but whenever they felt the need of refreshment — taking care to keep an eye on Amigo, and unload him at the right place. Never did a dog enjoy liberty and a bath more, and no sooner was his pack removed — a full pack, now, always — than he shot into the water or woods, and made the grand rounds, timing his returning nicely, so as to get back after the fire had been made and dinner or supper cooked. Perhaps he thought that he might be asked to fetch wood next if he wasn't careful, and took this way of getting out of it.

For the next month the children travelled in an easy, agreeable fashion, without cares or anxieties of any kind, and no very striking adventures. They had shade when they wanted it, and tramped many a mile under the leafy aisles of the woods that fringed the river. They had water at hand, and were not so much as obliged to fill their canteens unless they chose to do so; and as for food it had merely become a question what kind or kinds to select. Finding the game so plentiful, they gave up all idea of providing for future needs after a while, and left it to chance to supply their wants. They might have venison, ducks, pigeons, quail, turkeys, rabbits, squirrels, fish, and honey, whenever they pleased, to say nothing of berries — a state of affairs which was a decided improvement on certain past experience. Amigo wore his saddle, indeed, but had only the empty bags to carry, and made light of those.

Juan actually got too lazy to hunt deer, soon, and contented himself with the small game; but, to his credit be it said, he killed of this only what he needed, and did not take advantage of its plentifulness to wantonly slaughter whatever came in his way. He got very tired, though (so he told Nita), of shooting the same things every day, forgetting that, not long before, he would have been only too thankful to have anything to shoot. He said that what he wanted was some 'real sport.' The truth was that, having been thrown on his own resources and forced to use the brains and courage with which he had been originally endowed, he had grown so manly and self-reliant that, conscious of his mastery over nature, he longed for fresh opportunities to exercise the faculties that had been called into play by the circumstances of his flight from the Comanche camp.

When he saw the herds of buffalo in the distance, moving in wave-like undulations across the prairie, and blackening it for miles, he sighed afresh for the milk-white steed of his brightest imaginations, but would have been content with any well-trained horse on which to hunt the noble bison; and, had he possessed one, would, I am afraid, have postponed going back to Mexico until his thirst for excitement was somewhat quenched. Not that he knew anything about hunting buffalo. He had always been left in camp with the old warriors, squaws, and children, when the Indians went on their annual hunts; but he had long looked forward to the time when he would be allowed to join these expeditions, and his highest earthly ambition was to shoot a buffalo through the neck as Shaneco and Casteel did. So full was he of boyish daring that he felt ready to tackle almost anything now, and the need of tackling something grew more imperative every day.

At last, one day, when he and Nita were having breakfast on the roots of a pecan tree, in lieu of a table, he surprised his sister by saying that he didn't want any turkey — he was tired of turkey.

'Take some fish, then,' suggested Nita, unconscious of the underlying cause for discontent.

'I am tired of fish, too,' said Juan. 'I think I must look around and see if I can't find a nice, fat young bear. The ribs would be so good, roasted.'

'A bear! Oh, Juan!' exclaimed Nita. 'You are jesting, surely.'

All that day he brooded over the possibility of getting a bear, and convinced Nita that he was not jesting by saying suddenly, that afternoon (apropos of nothing that had gone before):

'We will roast it before a fire of mesquite coals, and it will be delicious.'

'Roast what?' she asked.

'That bear,' he replied.

Perhaps he only perversely longed for bear because it was the one animal that they had not seen so far. And, strange to say, that very evening, as they were walking along the river-bank, trying to settle upon a site for their camp, an old she-bear and two cubs came in sight, as if conjured up by Juan's ardent desire to see them. As a rule, bears only move late in the evening and early in the morning; and, knowing this, Juan ought to have been somewhat prepared for this encounter, especially as he had been rehearsing it in imagination for two days. But, as a matter of fact, he was taken completely aback, and stood stock-still and stared at Mrs. Bruin and her young ones, as though they had been elephants or giraffes, for fully sixty seconds, before it occurred to him to do anything except stare. Then he recovered himself, and hastily unsaddled Amigo, who looked alertly around him to see what was going to be hunted, and hoped it was another wolf, very likely, being vain of having once captured a lobos. Nita, being told to fit an arrow and come up closer, obeyed, nor once thought of deserting Juan, her love for him being much greater than her fears for herself. The trio presented a wonderfully brave front to the enemy. To be sure they had not the exaggerated fear of bears that civilized children have. Juan had often seen them killed by Indians; Amigo had often helped kill them; and even Nita knew that they were not likely to eat her up out of hand, and could be killed if an arrow was sent into the right place at the right moment.

So the hunters kept their presence of mind, and waited for the enemy to come within reach. Unconscious of the excitement she was creating, the old bear came slowly on and on, followed by her cubs, until she got nearly opposite the children, who were up on the bank, and partially concealed by the bushes growing there.

Down the bank sprang Juan and ran toward the bear, hissing Amigo on at the same moment. It was but little encouragement that Amigo needed, for he was used to the business; and, having already scented them, knew very well what was expected of him. Amazed by the sudden onslaught, Mrs. Bruin stood bolt upright on her hind feet, and stared in her turn at her foes.

She had never seen either a boy or a dog before; and, not caring to face the unknown, turned round, and took to her heels. The cubs followed her, and Amigo and the children gave chase.

Here was lively work for all parties concerned! In a few minutes Amigo left off nipping at the heels of the mother-bear and laid hold of one of the cubs, which bounded on for another moment, squawking with fifty-pig power, and then broke loose, rushed up the bank, and climbed up into a small tree.

More convinced than ever that she had to deal with the most terrible enemies, the old bear rushed along the river-bottom as fast as her clumsy legs could carry her, leaving her cubs to take care of themselves, intent alone on saving herself. When she had quite disappeared, the children eagerly ran up the bank; and, having reached the tree in which the cub had taken refuge, found Amigo sitting at the foot of it, barking furiously. He got up presently, and fairly danced around it, jumping up occasionally to snap at the cub's heels, which were barely out of reach, and hung down in a way that was enough to tantalize the most phlegmatic dog that ever went hunting, and excited Amigo beyond

THE CUB WAS SO TAKEN UP WITH THE DOG THAT HE HAD NO EYES
FOR JUAN AND NITA

measure. The cub was so taken up with the dog that he had no eyes for Juan and Nita, who crept up very close, and sent two arrows into him.

By this time Nita was so excited that she was no longer afraid of anything, but having discharged her arrow walked away a little distance. Juan did the same, and was standing near her, when all at once, the cub came tumbling out of the tree, losing all hold at once, bear-fashion, righted himself, and broke into a run, taking, by accident, the direction of the children. They, of course, took to their heels, Nita ahead. Amigo brought up the rear; and a more comical race was never seen, or one that finished more absurdly; for presently Nita stumbled and fell in the tall grass, Juan struck his foot against her, and went sprawling over her on all-fours, and the cub ran straight over both, more scared than either of them, with Amigo close to his heels.

The children picked themselves up. Amigo stuck to his work. The cub did not get far; he had two arrows in his lungs the ends of which kept striking against the bushes as he ran, and cutting him internally in a dreadful way. Amigo soon overtook him; but, badly wounded as he

was, he stood up on his hind legs, with his back
to the river-bank, and gave Amigo some terrible
blows with his paws. Seeing this, Juan and Nita
came running up and gave him a finishing shot.
Down he fell, and gave the most awful groans,
that sounded so human that Nita's hair almost
stood on end; but Juan was too proud of his success to think much of poor cubling's last utter-
ances, and only regretted that the other bears
had escaped him.

It was quite dark, and he determined to camp
where they were; so a big fire was lit, the cub
was butchered, and the children soon had the
meat cut off and distributed about in the nearest
bushes and the bones put upon sticks before the
blaze. As for the ribs they were roasted by mesquite coals, as Juan had decided they should be,
and were much enjoyed by the hungry hunters.
So fat, sweet, and tender was it, indeed, that
when supper was over the children took the
trouble to build a scaffold of sticks, and barbecue,
or rather dry, the remainder of the meat over a
slow fire, and, this done, betook themselves to
sleep.

Next morning Amigo was taken back to the
place where his saddle had been left, and then

brought to camp again, and loaded down with bear's meat, which he thought a poor return for the services he had rendered, and he carried it with an ill grace for several days.

This stirring experience furnished the travellers with a staple for both food and conversation, which lasted a long while; and Juan was always hoping that it would be repeated; but it never was. Every morning, when he was awakened by the gobble of turkeys, and the howling of the coyotes, Juan would reconnoitre the neighborhood in which he found himself, to see if there were any bear-tracks to be found, and every evening he would peer about him through the fast-deepening shadows about the camp, in the hope that luck would befriend him; but all in vain.

Another interval of monotonous marching now ensued, and then their progress came very near being arrested forever by a new and perfectly unforeseen danger. The weather had been unusually hot for several days, and they had felt it very much, for two reasons. Finding that the river they had been following veered decidedly away to the eastward, Juan had left it two days before, reluctantly enough, and had struck off southwest, into an open prairie, having previously provided himself with full canteens, and a good supply of food. The packs of all three travellers were proportionately heavy; and, in consequence, their weight was so oppressive, that, at noon on the day of which I am about to speak, Juan's patience gave out completely.

'I shall leave this great, hot, heavy thing here,' he said, giving the Mexican blanket, under which he had been staggering for an hour, an impatient little kick. 'I'll not carry it another step. What do we want with a blanket in the middle of the summer, anyway? I am sorry I ever started with it. I only did so because Shaneco always takes his, and all the other braves. Such nonsense!'

His face was crimson with his exertions, and he had worked himself up into a pretty temper, or rather an ugly one. Not all the water of the large pool near which they had stopped could cool his passion, and even his dinner failed to restore his usual good-nature.

'We can't stay here; there isn't a particle of shade,' he said crossly, when he had eaten sparingly, and drank of the tepid water; and, quite conscious that he was making Nita move on much against her will, he took an unhappy pleasure in making her as uncomfortable as himself. He carried out his threat about the blanket, too, throwing it down by the little lake in a heap, and then started off, with the most aggrieved expression in the world, across the prairie which seemed to fairly blaze in the afternoon sun.

He had gone only about a quarter of a mile when, suddenly, in less time than it takes to write this, a wind came rushing and roaring across the prairie, like a living thing, and changed him, and everything about him, with its first blast; an icy wind that set his very teeth chattering in five minutes, and in five more had chilled him to the bone — in short, the wind which all Texans know and dread — a 'norther.' No one who has not been caught out in one can form any idea of its swift descent, its terrible force, its bitter cold. An old Texan would not trust himself out on the prairies in July or August with the thermometer at ninety-six degrees, without two blankets strapped at his saddle-bow, to keep him from freezing to death in a norther, should one blow up, as it may do at any time; and even in the towns people are obliged to take to fires and winter clothing, while the Mexicans in Texas have such a dread of exposing themselves to it that, the moment one comes, they collect their children and dogs, and retire into their adobe huts, and are not seen again for three days, unless imperatively required to leave them.

It will be seen, then, that Juan and Nita were in a sufficiently serious position when that bitter blast swept down from the regions of perpetual ice and snow, and found them in the most exposed position possible, in mid-prairie. The shock dissipated Juan's fretfulness, of course, at once, but replaced it with the gravest anxiety. He looked desperately about him for a moment, to see if there was any shelter to be found, but there was none. Neither cliff, nor cave, nor wood was within reach, the nearest approach to the latter being some straggling bushes of mesquite, quite half a mile away.

'Back! Let us run back!' he cried, and turned again toward the lake, to seek his despised blanket. Shivering with mingled cold and fear, Nita raced along by his side without a word; and Amigo, as conscious of the sudden change in the atmosphere as either of them, and as alarmed by it, distanced both, whining out his misgivings in a melancholy minor key. Fortunately there had been no other travellers passing that way, and the blanket was just where it had been left, so that Juan and Nita were soon rolled up into a sort of ball under it, with every particle of air excluded, as close to the prairie as they could get.

There they stayed for an hour; and then it occurred to Juan that the only shelter to be had was in the very bosom of mother-earth itself, and that, unless he meant to freeze outright in the course of the night, which was fast coming on, he must bestir himself. Accordingly, he told Nita that they must dig a hole there; and, without losing a moment, they raised themselves and proceeded to scoop out the earth at their feet with an energy, not to say frenzy, born of their desperate need. Will it be believed that Amigo no sooner saw what they were doing, than he, too, fell to scratching away frantically in the rear? And, though he was pushed aside by Juan soon, I have, personally, not the smallest doubt that he understood the situation perfectly, and could have rendered valuable aid had he been allowed to do so. The children felt a good deal warmer by the time they had been digging, hand over hand, for an hour, and in another hour had hollowed out quite a deep pit, smaller, no doubt, than the one into which Joseph was cast by his brethren, but big enough to bring their heads well below the level of the prairie when they finally crawled in. There was room for Amigo, too, of which he was glad to avail himself; and the three huddled close together for the sake of the warmth to be got from each other, and covered themselves, first with their blanket, and then partially with earth.

Here they were, to a certain extent, protected from the cruel wind that continued to sweep pitilessly across the prairie above them; but, even so, they were terribly cold and cramped from lying in one position, and scarcely slept at all. If Amigo had not been a sort of canine stove, that radiated heat without requiring any fuel the whole night long, the chances are that the children would have perished. As it was, they were very miserable, and were not in a mood to enjoy the magnificent sunrise that greeted them next morning. The sun rose, clear and brilliant, from a bed of gold, and seemed about to ascend his throne and wield his sceptre with his usual force. Juan was delighted to see him, and foolishly counted upon his routing the norther by noon of that day. He told Nita as much, but she only shivered, and burrowed a little farther down under the blanket, when, with a view to getting some breakfast, he wriggled judiciously out of his place and got his head above ground once more, only to have it nearly taken off the next moment — at least so it seemed to him, as the knife-like blast whistled past his ears.

On leaping out of the pit he found the lake, from which he had drunk tepid water not seventeen hours before, covered with a coating of ice, which he broke in order to fill his canteen. He then got some food from his wallet, and, with aching fingers and a thoroughly chilled body, crept back into the pit again, and, together with Nita and Amigo, swallowed his breakfast as best he could.

Noon came; but the norther still held the sun by the throat, and would not let so much as one ray drop to earth without passing through the icy medium it had prepared. Evening came, and the sun retired, defeated. Night brought an increase of cold, and was very dark and endless. The children left the pit to get their dinner and supper, and Amigo frisked briskly about to improve his circulation; but all three were thankful to crawl back into it again.

And so passed three nights and three days, which seemed to the children, accustomed to a life of incessant activity, and practically buried alive for the time being, a month at least. Then the norther retired to the North Pole, as suddenly as it had come, and they were safe. The fourth night they did not suffer at all, and on the fifth day the sun had it all his own way. By noon on the sixth day it was midsummer temperature again, and the children resumed their journey, much subdued in spirit, and not quite so sure that they had dominated the mysterious forces which are summed up in Nature.

CHAPTER XI

COCK-CROW AND DAY DAWNS

LITTLE as they suspected it, the children were only about seventy-five miles from the Texan frontier when they were overtaken by that norther. I am not sure whether it would have made them more or less impatient of confinement and delay to know it; but, again released, they went blundering along in perfect ignorance of their whereabouts. The first thing that gave Juan the least suspicion of the fact was that the game grew steadily scarcer and wilder from the time they left the river. It occurred to him, however, that this might only mean that the Indians were there, or had been there; so he said nothing to Nita about it, and kept a bright lookout.

The very last flock of wild turkeys that they saw was in the woodland that they struck after crossing the open prairie. They reached it toward nightfall, camped, and were sitting quietly over the fire, where some meat was being warmed up, when the turkeys came in to roost, and again perched fearlessly over their heads in the branches of two cottonwoods. Juan listened approvingly as he heard them settling into their places, meaning to 'settle' one or two of them in a different way when he had appeased his hunger; but, while he was still eating, there came a sound of great fluttering among the turkeys, and flapping of wings. Out charged Amigo, always ready to accept a challenge of any kind, and they soon heard him fighting some invisible animal. 'He has got the best of it,' said Juan; 'for I hear him barking up a tree. Let us see what is up.'

Together he and Nita turned out, and came upon Amigo, much excited, and still barking, his eyes fixed intently upon something in the tree he was guarding. Juan made a little circuit, seeing this, and crept up in the rear, quite close, from which spot he got a good view of a large wild-cat, sitting up on a limb, and looking down at Amigo, growling and showing its teeth savagely. So completely absorbed was the cat in Amigo's barkings and boundings that it did not see Juan at all, or notice his flank movement, near as he was, until an arrow whizzed into its side, just behind the shoulder, when it sprang high in the air, and came down on the ground with a tremendous thud, mortally wounded. Thinking the battle over, and the victory won,

Amigo pounced eagerly on the cat, and had a very nice map of Texas scratched on his face in the few minutes the cat lived, but all the same was convinced that the triumph was his, and looked jubilant and vainglorious as he followed the children back to camp. Nita admired the skin of the cat so much that she persuaded Juan to save and stretch it, and they spent a good deal of time on it, using it finally to ornament Amigo's pack-saddle.

This was their last stirring adventure. They had not seen a buffalo, now, for weeks, or a deer for ten days; and the small game, as I have said, gave evidence of having been hunted, so that it became again no easy matter to get food. Water they did not lack, for they came upon two or three creeks, and managed to keep their canteens well filled, as a rule; but something to eat became the great question as they went on. A quail or a fox-squirrel was now a boon to them, and they would really have suffered again had not Amigo's hunger sharpened his wits, and led him to turn his attention to rabbits, which he ran into holes, and corners, and hollow trees, continually, and nabbed occasionally. But this was but a precarious subsistence; and so it came about that the children went supperless to bed at the close of a long, fatiguing march, one evening, feeling particularly depressed and exhausted. Even the canteens were now as empty as themselves, and they had no idea where they were, and the prospect for the future was sufficiently gloomy.

Altogether they had never felt more thoroughly depressed and perplexed than when they lay down patiently, side by side, in a certain little dell, at dusk on the 18th of August, 1875. They were so tired that they fell into a doze, from which they were aroused by Amigo. He was couched near them as usual, and awakened them rudely enough by springing up, and growling and barking furiously, all his hair bristling about him, and all the dog in him excited to the highest pitch. Up rose Juan, and promptly administered a cuff.

It was all very well for Amigo to give warning if danger impended, but it was stupid to make such a row as that, and attract attention. Forced to keep quiet, he still stood there, quivering with excitement; and the children looking about them with all their eyes, and listening with all their ears, now heard a faint, very distant, but unmistakable sound — that of a dog barking. Listen as they might, they heard nothing more, and that ceased after awhile, when Amigo became tranquil again, and the children lay down.

'It is the Indians,' affirmed Nita positively, and quaked afresh with fear.

'It may be the whites,' hazarded Juan, more to reassure her than anything else.

But that bark made it impossible for either of them to sleep. Broad awake were they the whole night, and feared, and hoped, and discussed many things, and waited with impatience for daylight and certainty to come. When it was barely light they rose, and walked rapidly on, keeping near the shelter of the wood, in case it should be necessary to conceal themselves suddenly from Comanches or Apaches, and so sustained by excitement as to be hardly aware of the fact that their long fast was still unbroken.

On they hurried, and would have continued to hurry, had they not suddenly been arrested by another sound, which had upon them much the same effect as though they had stumbled upon an electric battery fully charged. And what was it that came to them, clear, distinct, and apparently quite near, on the still morning air? Only the crow of a cock. Only the crow of a cock, do I say? Only home, love, joy, liberty, and all that is sweetest in life! They were safe! They had reached the settlements! They would soon be in their mother's arms! Is it any wonder that they stopped as suddenly as though they had been shot, turned pale as little ghosts, gave a shriek that ought to have penetrated to the *hacienda,* and threw themselves weeping on each other's breasts, where they embraced, and laughed, and sobbed, and gesticulated, and danced about like the frantic, wild things they were?

And then how they did run toward that blessed, blessed cock, with might and main, and heart and soul, and a speed that they had never equalled, not even when the fear of death, not love, lent wings to their feet! They raced on until they were perfectly breathless; and, then, perforce, ran slower and slower, astonished not to see further evidences of civilization, deceived, as many an older person has been, in regard to the distance a cock can be heard at dawn.

They were obliged to subside into a walk at last, if the hurried, buoyant, joyous tread with which they got over that prairie can be called a walk; Amigo, perfectly comprehending that something delightful had happened, bounding along beside them, all frisks and wags and laughing content. It had seemed so near, only a few hundred yards away. But it was two miles, and, to their burning, consuming impatience, it seemed two hundred. Up came the sun to see the charming spectacle that awaited him; and there — yes, there was a road, newly travelled, assurance doubly sure! And there was a house! And a garden! And in that garden a white man! Oh, joy! Oh, rapture!

Transported with delight, the children rushed down that road, leaped over that fence, and rushed up to that white man, crying out, 'Señor! Señor!' in accents of frenzied ecstasy. At least they rushed *toward* him. They did not get up to him, for the simple reason that he no sooner caught sight of them than he, too, made a rush, but in the opposite direction; and, although he was an immensely stout, unwieldy man, he got into his own house, and barricaded the door, almost as quickly as though he had been the slimmest youth or professional athlete, so alarmed was he by what he believed to be the advance guard of a party of Indians.

The children, left standing in the midst of his neat rows of beans and melons, stared blankly in the direction in which he had disappeared, completely confounded for the moment by his behavior. It had never occurred to them that their satisfaction at seeing a civilized being again would not be shared by him. But the pleasure was anything but mutual.

They had made their way by chance to one of the cabins that (surrounded by small farms) formed the fringe of the German settlement near Fredericksburg — a settlement on which the Indians frequently made raids, and in which a Comanche was more dreaded than anything in the world; and they had given a terrible fright to a worthy Teuton, who had taken himself, his excellent wife, and seven blue-eyed, flaxen-polled children out there to subdue the wilderness, and make it blossom like the rose, or, rather, like their beloved 'Vaterland.'

For the past six months the Indians had left them in peace; and when the industrious head of an industrious family had turned out at daylight that morning to work in his garden, he had gone armed only with his hoe and a powder for killing the striped bug which had attacked his melons. Great had been the horror, then, of Mr. Conrad Braun at the descent of the supposed savages; and, once indoors, he lost no time in arming himself and his boys, and shutting and bolting and barring every door and window, in expectation of a siege.

'They are afraid! Afraid of us!' exclaimed Nita, in excessive astonishment. She was much more used to feeling terrified than to inspiring terror, and could not understand how she could alarm any one.

'They take us for Indians,' replied Juan. 'We must undeceive them. But don't go too near the house, Nita. You will be shot before I can make them understand, if you are not careful.'

Thus warned, Nita dropped into the background, and Juan went forward a little. Mr. Braun, who was reconnoitering at a peep-hole, saw him distinctly, and only waited for him to come a little nearer to shoot. But Juan stopped, puzzled how to explain the situation by pantomime, and the next moment had picked up a small, white garment that Frau Braun had left out on the grass to bleach overnight, and had stuck it on a stick. With the flag-of-truce he had improvised, he walked toward the house again, taking care not to run any risks, and waved his stick vigorously, crying out, '*Amigos! Amigos!*' again and again. But, unfortunately, the Indians had done the same thing in one of their forays, as a ruse to gain admittance to a house in that very neighborhood, and had subsequently butchered its inmates; so that Mr. Braun's suspicions, so far from being allayed, were strongly confirmed by Juan's conduct. He remained behind his stout, wooden shutters, gun in hand, and had no idea of being taken in by any such device.

As for Juan he knew that it would never do to follow his impulse, and approach the house. He dared not move another foot toward it, and got angry at being mistaken for an Indian, and could not hit upon a plan of action. At last he threw down his bow and quiver, and, holding up his hands, ran down the path that led to the front door, shouting out, '*Mexicanos! Mexicanos! Captivos de los Indios! Amigos! Amigos!*'

Luckily for him Mr. Braun understood Spanish. He had been a baker in San Antonio for some years, and had learned it there. He was by no means sure, though, that this might not be another Indian ruse, and meant to make no fatal mistake; so he waited for a very long while on the right side of his door, while Juan banged impatiently on the other, and repeated vehemently his explanation.

Finally, after a long parley, he peeped and peered all about the yard, and, not seeing anything in the shape of a grown Indian, began to slowly and cautiously unbolt and unbar. He had previously repeated and translated what Juan had said, to his wife, who was wholly unconvinced by what she considered specious fictions, and gave a great shriek when she saw what her spouse was going to do. 'Thou wilt be killed, Conrad, and our loved children! *Ach Himmel!*' she cried, and snatched up as many children as she could, expecting to see a dozen savages pour into the room through the opening door. Hearing this, Mr. Braun repented of his rashness, and shut the door suddenly again, in Juan's very face. Finding, however, that nothing dreadful succeeded — nothing of any kind, indeed — he plucked up courage to open it again, a little wider this time. He held it in his hand ready to clap it to the instant he saw anything to alarm him; but he saw only Juan, who kept on repeating that he was an Indian captive, but not an Indian — a Mexican, on the contrary.

Fully reassured at last, Mr. Braun changed his tactics completely. He flung wide the door; he shouted to his wife: 'It is true, Hanna! Come

thou here.' He seized Juan, and would have
dragged him bodily into the house, had not that
agile young person slipped like an eel from his
large grasp back into the path, and called to his
sister to join him, in eager, delighted tones. She
obeyed; shrank back, abashed for a moment, on
seeing the whole Braun family assembled there;
caught Juan's eye, and walked with him indoors.
Benevolent, large-hearted Frau Braun, rid of all
fear for the safety of her husband and children
and (incidentally) herself, was at once all excitement and emotion, and had her ready sympathies
diverted into another channel. Her broad, mild
face radiated the vivid and kindly interest that
she felt; and her motherly heart went out at once
to the haggard, tattered, way-worn children before her, though she little knew what cause she
had to pity them.

'Indian captives? So?' she said. 'Escaped,
you said, Conrad? Sit here, sit here!' (To the
children.) 'Tell us of it — But, no! not now.
Rest first; you are tired.'

She pushed two stools toward Juan and Nita
as she spoke, and continued to regard them with
the friendliest eyes; but they took no notice of
her offer. They had not seen anything in the

shape of a chair, since they left the *hacienda;* and, while they understood her gesture, felt much embarrassed by the proposition, and quickly dropped down on the floor, near each other, in cross-legged comfort.

Mr. Braun, acting as interpreter, now took a seat, and began to question Juan. The Braun children formed in a semicircle, and stared at Juan and Nita, as only children, and country-children at that, can stare; the good Frau took her little Conradchen on her knee, and prepared to listen. Nine pairs of large, blue eyes got bigger every moment, as Juan briefly and simply told his story, and one pair overflowed with pitying tears more than once during its recital.

Frau Braun rocked violently backward and forward, and clasped her baby more closely in her arms, as she heard how these little Mexicans had been torn away from their mother. Over their subsequent sufferings among the Indians, the escape and journey, she wept copiously, and sighed profoundly, calling 'the loved God' and 'the loved Heaven' to witness in frequent ejaculations that there had never been anything like it. And when Juan told of the cock-crow, and of his joy at finding himself among white people again, and his wish to go back to the *hacienda* as soon as possible, Frau Braun got up impulsively, shifted Conradchen to the left arm, and, sinking down on her knees by Juan and Nita, she encircled both of them with the right, in a warm embrace; and, without a moment's hesitation, kissed the dirty, brown faces that were turned toward her in wondering astonishment.

Her husband only half believed what he had been told. It was incredible that any two children could have safely accomplished such a journey, to his mind; so he made no demonstrations of any kind. The Frau accepted it as truth at once, and her motherly heart yearned over them inexpressibly. It was a relief to her feelings to set about getting them a good breakfast; and she laid the baby in his cradle, and set to work at once, with this object in view. Her husband returned to the garden and his vegetables; the little Brauns broke ranks somewhat, but continued to indulge in absorbed stares from every part of the room; and as for Juan and Nita they found occupation enough for their eyes when left to themselves. They were in a house, which was in itself a novel and striking fact; and, cabin as it was, that house was full of the most interest-

ing objects to them. There was a bed in the
corner, for one thing, and the brother and sister
exchanged glances over it. They had not seen a
bed for many a long day; and there were a table,
and chairs, and a fireplace, and pots, and pans,
and kettles, and buckets, and other household
effects, and a woman bustling about almost as if
she were the Señora. So strongly were they reminded of their mother by the Frau, although
there was no resemblance between them, except
that of womanly kindness and general motherli-
ness, that the tears rose to Nita's eyes, and she
whispered to Juan:

'Don't stay here. Let us go home as soon as
we can.'

'*Si! Si!*' assented Juan, and nodded; and then
both found a new attraction in the baby, which
was cooing, and kicking, and gurgling, and smiling at them, not two feet away — a baby that
promised to be a shade larger and fairer than any
of its brothers or sisters, with even bluer eyes,
and pretty little yellow curls escaping from under
its close, German cap.

When breakfast was ready, one of the boys
ran out to the well and brought in a pail of fresh
water, part of which he spilled on the floor, in

consequence of the necessity he was under of looking at Juan and Nita instead of noticing what he was about; and another, being told to call his father, ran to the back door and gave his voice, indeed, to his work, but scarcely removed his eyes for one moment from the fascinating strangers in the corner.

Mr. Braun being come, the family seated themselves at table. With instinctive politeness the good housewife had not laid a place for the Mexican children, and did not ask them to come to the table; but she seized two big plates, and perhaps she did not pile them high with smoking meats, and vegetables, and hominy, and bread! And, not content with this, she went over to a cupboard, and added a smaller heap of preserves, and a huge slice of seed-cake, and even some of her very best sweet pickle. This last, by the by, was pushed aside as soon as tasted, condiments being unpleasant to these palates; and, with a plate apiece in front of them, Juan and Nita left their knives and forks to serve an ornamental purpose, and furnished such effective substitutes, in the way of fingers, that everything was soon ravenously snatched up and disposed of, the little Brauns watching the performance with unflagging interest. The plates were again filled by the smiling Frau, and again emptied by the hungry children, who unceremoniously threw their discarded bones down on the floor, filled their hands with hominy to be conveyed in bulk to their mouths, and displayed generally ˋComanche table-manners.

As for Amigo no one who knows him can suppose for one moment that he had not shared in all that had happened; the reception accorded his young master and mistress, the morning *séance* or rather court of inquiry, and, most important of all, the breakfast. He had bounded into the cabin with Nita, snuffed searchingly at every member of the Braun family, made the rounds of the room to see what it was like, and had then consented to be patted by Mr. Braun, after which he curled up on the floor at Juan's feet, having satisfied himself that all was well, and so returned to that civilization of which he was a bright ornament, as well-bred and far more accomplished than when he left it at the call of duty. *He* was not roughened by contact with rough people; nothing could make a savage of *him*. He was at home alike in the finest drawing-room or an Indian lodge, and would have shone as conspicuously in the best society as in the worst. He now ignored the life he had been obliged to lead for several years, and, being out of the woods, relapsed, with easy grace, into the habits and manners of polite life.

He was quite tall enough to have made a snatch at the tempting steaks and corn-muffins that graced his host's board; but, as a matter of fact, what did he do? Why, he walked around the circle assembled there, quietly at first, merely to be on hand if he were wanted. And then he looked with intention and expectation, now at one, now at another member of the family. And then, surprised to find himself rudely neglected, he stood on his hind legs, and laid one paw in remonstrance on Mr. Braun's arm, merely to recall him to a sense of what was due a guest from a host. And then, being given an immense bone, he gracefully expressed his thanks in the only way open to him by repeated wags of his handsome tail, and retired politely out of doors with it that he might not get so much as one spot of grease on Frau Braun's neatly-scrubbed floor — conduct that defies criticism and challenges admiration in a courtier, much more in a dog that had eaten nothing for more than twenty-four hours, and spent the best years of his life among the Comanches — such is the force of native superiority, and its power to rise above misfortune. Never can it be said after this that 'Circumstances make the dog' — they only make the man.

All during the stay of the travellers with the Brauns, Amigo's behavior kept on this high level. He was perfectly simple, natural, affable, gave himself no airs of superiority, demanded no sympathy for past triumphs or sufferings, and managed, moreover, to endear himself to all with whom he was thrown. He must have been singularly attractive; for, several times that day, the youthful Brauns actually averted their eyes from Juan and Nita for a moment, in order to look at him, which was more than their mother had been able to effect, although she had given them many a nudge and frown, intended to convey the idea that they had goggled long enough at the Indian captives.

Not content with having satisfied the wants of the inner man, or, rather, child, Frau Braun's mind was full of schemes for improving the outer Mexican. All the while that she was attending to her daily duties she was revolving certain pos-

sibilities, mentally trying to determine whether
Hans's coat and Carl's trousers would fit Juan,
although Hans was a good deal bigger, and Carl
as much smaller, than her protégé; and whether
her Faustina's clothes would do for Nita. The
tattered buckskin garments, the dirty faces, and
matted locks of the pair before her were such a
contrast to the condition of her own cleanly, fair,
rosy brood that she could scarcely wait until she
had finished certain household duties to get at the
family wardrobe and see what it would furnish
forth.

Before entering upon the work of the day Mr.
Braun rejoiced Juan's heart by telling him that
he was going to San Antonio shortly, and would
take them that far on their road to Mexico —
news that made his large brown eyes sparkle
with delight, and caused Nita to literally jump
for joy. It further appeared that Mr. Braun was
collecting a load of pecans to take with him, and
meant to take a goodly store of honey, butter,
and eggs, as well, to that market. He asked the
children whether they would like to help him,
and they did like; and, accompanied by our two
Mexicans and six out of seven of his offspring,
he started out into the woods, where they all

stayed until dinner-time, and gathered bushels of nuts, which they brought home and deposited under the shed back of the house.

In the course of this process some advance toward acquaintance, if not intimacy, had naturally been made between the German and Mexican children. With the freemasonry of youth, and a few words and signs, they managed to get on very well in their joint labors, and a good understanding was inaugurated — enough to take the edge off the Braun stare, at all events, and make Juan and Nita feel more at home.

All that afternoon Frau Braun had her enormous work-basket beside her, and diligently sewed upon various garments previously shaped by her immense shears; and by evening, lo! a neat, if not particularly stylish, outfit for Juan, and another for Nita! This done, she prepared baths in the two rooms overhead, set apart for her boys and for her girls; and, calling to Mr. Braun, arranged the next step in her admirable programme. The result was that even Amigo scarcely knew his own master and mistress at supper that night. They had been tubbed, and scrubbed, and rubbed; their hair had been shaved off close to the scalp; their clothes thrown away; and themselves inducted into a full suit of garments, remarkable in cut, indeed; altered, patched, but as clean as soap and water could make them. They scarcely knew themselves or each other in this guise, but were infinitely refreshed, and as comfortable as they could be in civilized clothes, which seemed to them to be constructed on painfully rigid and constraining principles, and to be unnecessarily numerous and very gorgeous. It was well, perhaps, that the small Brauns wore their feet *au naturel*, and that no attempt was made to put Juan and Nita into stockings and stiff shoes just then. Not all their gratitude to the people who had so kindly received them could have stood such a test, I fear.

And how Frau Braun did beam at them when she seated them with her own children around the tea-table! And how she did butter their corn-bread, and set a great bowl of bread-and-milk before each of them! And how kind Mr. Braun was! And how Hans, and Gustave, and Carl, and Albert, and Faustina, and Bertha, and Wilhelmina Christine did behave themselves, to be sure! And what were Nita's sensations at finding herself lying once more under a roof, and in a bed, between sheets! She dropped off to sleep before she had time to properly realize how cool, and soft, and clean, and deliciously comfortable it was, which was a pity, and she slept until Frau Braun called her next morning, and took ten minutes then to get her eyes really open.

But it was different with Juan. He tried conscientiously to stay where he was put, and tried to get to sleep, and only tumbled and tossed, and tossed and tumbled. He could not stand sleeping in a bed. That was the trouble. It suffocated him, somehow; and at last he stole downstairs and outside, where he stretched himself out under the trees, and took an express train to the land of nod. There Frau Braun found him, much to her surprise, when she went out to do her milking, and couldn't understand it; and her husband, coming out of the house just then, saw it too, and shook his fat sides with laughter over it for fully ten minutes.

CHAPTER XII

AT LAST!

THE children could not understand why it was that they felt so dull and drowsy all the following day; so indisposed to do anything; so thoroughly tired and spent. It was that, like Shaneco's bow, they were unstrung, and, after the long tension of every faculty and feeling, required rest imperatively. Frau Braun, however, rightly interpreted their languor and air of torpidity. It was by her request that they were left behind when her husband and his boys started off nutting; and it was no surprise to her to see them sleep away the greater part of the day.

Even Amigo felt the need of *meditation*. He did not like to be accused of losing consciousness altogether, and always opened one eye when anybody said in his hearing that he was asleep. He certainly stretched himself out full-length on the grass in front of the cabin after breakfast for half an hour, wagged 'Good-bye, and great success' to the departing Brauns as they passed him, but made no move to accompany them; and then, feeling himself free from curious observa-

tion, curled around comfortably in his favorite
position, and did not move for two hours. After
this he rose, and stretched himself in two mo-
tions, fore-paws well down, and hind legs stiff,
first; and then fore-paws made suddenly very
rigid, and hind legs allowed to drag a little way
limply, yawning all the while prodigiously. But
of course he had not been asleep. Oh, dear, no!
not at all! I am sure he would have denied it
with his most emphatic bark if such a thing had
been suggested.

On the third day all the travellers were
brighter, and went off to the woods with the
Brauns, where Juan's skill in bringing down
birds and squirrels set the Braun children staring
worse than ever. Phlegmatic as they were in
temperament, their interest, curiosity, and admiration grew and intensified every hour and day
after that. Association with Juan and Nita became the most precious of their privileges; and,
to secure it, they shirked every duty possible,
and cheerfully abandoned all their former pur-
suits, games, and pets. Even their white rabbit,
a possession that had been held priceless, and had
only been brought to them the month before,
from San Antonio, was so utterly neglected that

it would have starved but for their mother's care, so absorbing was the new attraction. Hans and Carl got a beating apiece from their father for failing to bring the water and cut the wood as usual, and had long sentences poured upon them, so full of guttural wrath that any other than German boys would certainly have fled before them. Faustina and Wilhelmina had not swept because they 'couldn't find the broom anywhere,' and had not washed the dishes 'because the boys had not brought the water.'

Even the heads of the house felt the force of the new influence. Mr. Braun spent a good deal of time in questioning, requestioning, and cross-questioning Juan, that might have been given with advantage to his vegetables, and his wife forgot all about the bread on baking-day, and let it burn in the oven to a thick, black crust, while Juan's adventures were being translated for her benefit.

The story was told over and over again, for their benefit, for the benefit of credulous or incredulous neighbors, who, hearing wonderful tales of what was going on at the Brauns, rode up in great numbers for a sparse settlement, hitched their horses to the fence, came in, took off a yellow sun-bonnet, or a *sombrero*, as the case might be, seated themselves, and showed pretty plainly that they had come for the day, claiming Frau Braun's hospitality as freely as they would have granted it had the case been reversed.

When these worthy people had got into rush-bottomed chairs, and had refused or accepted 'a bite of somedings' — which was the Frau's adaptation of a local phrase, covering a wide range of refreshment — Juan and Nita (variously designated as 'them Injun children,' and 'them little greasers that got away from the Comanches') were summoned, and gave testimony.

Sometimes it was a German neighbor who appeared on the scene, and was received with effusion by the family, especially by Mr. Braun, who seemed to feel that every man of them was a brother, and would clasp them affectionately to his ample bosom, kiss them on each cheek, and produce lager-beer and pipes before they had been in the house ten minutes. When the air was thick with smoke and German adjectives, Juan and Nita were sent for, that seeing might be believing, all explanation being necessarily left to Mr. Braun.

At last, one day, an old Texan came, who said
he wouldn't ''light'; threw a leg over the pom-
mel of his saddle; let an eye as cool as a toad's
rest on Juan, while he told the story; asked a good
many leading questions; chewed meditatively
while he listened to the replies; and then summed
up his conclusions in 'I'm blamed if he ain't
tellin' the truth!' Having thus given his official
sanction to a tale that sadly lacked confirmation
to many minds, he nodded to such Brauns as
were about, stuck his spurs in his mustang, and
rode away again, leaving Juan's credit above
par, to use a commercial phrase, for he was the
great authority of that part of the State on such
matters. He had lived among the Comanches,
had been an Indian scout and guide for thirty
years, and knew the country over which the
children had passed as well as any Indian of
them all.

It took a week for Mr. Braun to collect all the
things that he wished to take to San Antonio;
and it is likely that he would not have got off
then but for the assistance that Juan rendered.
He electrified and fascinated the boys by finding
and skilfully robbing two bee-caves, and pleased
their thrifty father as well by this exercise of

woodcraft; and, as for pecans, he could find, thresh, shake, gather them as no other boy had ever been known to do. The covered wagon in which the proposed journey was to be made was piled so high with them that there was scarcely room for anything else, or anybody. Not unaware of the admiration he had excited in the breasts of the little Brauns, Juan did his best, and we know how good that was. He was not above showing them what he could do with Shaneco's bow, for one thing; and you could almost have hung your hat on Faustina's protruding eyes when Nita strung her little bow one day, and brought down a wild turkey. It was heartbreaking to think of giving up such delightful guests, not to mention Amigo, whose packsaddle alone was a joy forever. They would have saddled and unsaddled him from morning until night all that week but for parental interference; and, as it was, Amigo was obliged to make a stand about it.

At last the day came for leaving, and the high-shouldered wagon rolled away from the door with a very miscellaneous load of nuts, honey, butter, chickens, and children, Mr. Braun driving, Amigo looking over his shoulder to see that he

did the thing properly. Six inconsolable Braun-
lings, defeated in as many efforts apiece to join
the party, hung over the fence and swarmed
about the wheels to the last. One of them appeared suddenly around the corner of the canvas
hood-cover, just as they started, and thrust upon
Nita the white rabbit. A good woman, with a
child in her arms, stood on 'the doorstep, and
wept as she called down a last blessing upon
Juan and Nita, and predicted that they would
soon be with their mother. Mr. Braun gave a
tremendous crack with his long whip, and they
were off.

The children had been wholly glad to think
that morning that they were to enter upon
another stage of their journey, and were to be
taken, without any effort or anxiety or care of
their own, to a place where Mexicans abounded,
from which they could easily be sent back to
Santa Rosa. But the overflowings of mother-
love even, had so softened hearts long used to
cruelty and neglect, or, at best, indifference,
that they could not but cling to Frau Braun; and
now, as the brother and sister sat there, the tears
streamed down both faces, although Juan made
desperate efforts to control what he considered a

disgraceful weakness. 'What would Shaneco think if he could see me *crying!*' he thought, and choked down the lump in his throat, and dried his eyes as soon as possible.

In some ways that short journey was as trying to them as any they had undergone lately. They were in no danger, they knew, and were sure to have all their wants provided for; but they were perched so high on the chicken-coops that they constantly knocked their heads against the hoops that supported the wagon-cover; the heat was intense, the confinement almost insupportable after the free, active life they had led. It seemed to them that Mr. Braun's sorry team was a perfect failure as a means of locomotion (and, indeed, their owner rarely cared to urge them into a mild trot even); and the children were sure that they could get over the ground as fast or faster, yet dared not suggest any change in the arrangement made.

That first day was a trial to them. They crossed that loveliest of streams, the Guadaloupe, that evening, and camped on the other side; and what a relief it was to get out of that close wagon, and be able to move about freely again! It was a pleasure to water the horses;

and Juan was interested in the harness, the like of which he had never seen; and Nita got wood, and made a fire, and then fed the chickens in the coops; and Mr. Braun cooked an excellent supper, and, having enjoyed it, sat down to smoke, bidding the children play until they were tired, and then go to bed under the wagon, where they would be protected from dew or rain — a new idea to them.

Next morning Juan was allowed to play postilion, and mounted the right-hand leader, a serious old roan, not much like the Indian ponies to which he was accustomed, but preferable to the coop, on the whole, as a riding-animal. And Nita was invited to sit in front with Mr. Braun, which was a great improvement; and she tried her hand at driving a bit, and wondered why civilized people went about in cumbersome, heavy vehicles tied by innumerable straps to such horses, instead of riding spirited mustangs, as the Comanches did.

About midday they crossed the Cibolo, and that evening, from the hills northwest of San Antonio, were looking down upon the city of the Alamo — a fortress once so nobly defended against overwhelming odds that, as a great soldier has said of it, 'Marathon and Thermopylæ had their messengers, but the Alamo had none!' The town gleamed whitely in the heart of a beautiful valley — the valley of its own beautiful river — a green sweep of verdure at that distance, with the fine old dome of the Spanish Mission Cathedral, La Concepcion, beyond, clearly outlined against a blue sky.

'Oh, Juan! *Mira! Mira! Casas! Casas! Casas!*' exclaimed Nita, who had never seen as many houses in her life before, and was in a great state of excitement.

'There are Mexicans there,' said homesick Juan.

'I hope butter has gone up,' said Mr. Braun, and turned his horses' heads toward a little stream, where he meant to camp for the night.

It was most disappointing to the children to stop at all with the city actually in sight; but Mr. Braun had his own views on the subject, and was not to be persuaded into changing them. Butter might have gone down for aught he knew, and the horses were tired, and he was in no special hurry to reach town; so Juan and Nita had to resign themselves to the inevitable as best they could — which was as follows — by playing in the clear waters of the San Ignacio, wandering among its groves, and catching enough perch and catfish for supper.

The next morning they drove at quite a rattling pace down into the city, and came to a full stop on the Military or Grand Plaza — a great square, one side of which is taken up by a mellow old cathedral with an imposing façade and beautiful dome; the other three by hotels, stores, and private houses, having a flagstaff in the middle, about which numbers of other wagons, *caritas*, vehicles of all kinds were grouped, and about these, booths, stalls, long tables piled high with *tamales*, *tortillas*, *peloncillos*, and around these, again, mountains of watermelons, in charge of the most Mexican Mexicans this side of the Rio Grande. The sight of them, and of the cathedral, and the plaza generally, filled the children with rapture. It was all so familiar that they stood as in a dream for a moment after they left the wagon, gazing at the *burros* near them, so loaded with hay that nothing was visible of them but their long ears, and four feet, as like the donkeys of Santa Rosa as possible; at the hairless dogs that raced past them, the dogs of Santa Rosa; at the shovel-hatted, cassocked priest, just entering the flat-roofed *adobe* house opposite, who might easily have been mistaken for Padre Garcia in Santa Rosa; in short, at the miniature Mexico into which they had dropped.

Mr. Braun, in his best German-Spanish, was soon giving the history of Juan and Nita; and to the chronic idlers of the plaza were added men, women, children, in ever-increasing numbers, until the wagon was completely surrounded by an eager, excited crowd, that hung upon every word that proceeded from his lips. An impulsive and tender-hearted people, they were touched to the quick by what they heard; they wept, they laughed, they cheered, exclaimed, gesticulated, wept again, seized Mr. Braun's hands and kissed them, embraced now Juan, now Nita, ardently, and were shaken by a tempest of emotion such as colder races cannot understand.

The story flew; the story grew, and so did the crowd. Everybody wanted to see the hero and heroine of such tremendous adventures. Everybody wanted to entertain them, caress them, comfort them, help them. There never was a prettier uproar. Every mother there seemed to see one of her own brown babies in the Indian captives; every man's heart burned within him,

at the thought of their sufferings; the shovel-
hatted Padre pressed forward to give them his
blessing; the shrill, nasal chatter of the babbling
crowd rose to a shriek; the babies, exposed to a
hot sun, cried; the very dogs took part in the
demonstration, and barked, and fought, and in-
sinuated themselves everywhere.

A Mexican of prominence stepped forward,
and assumed the temporary guardianship of the
bewildered children, and Mr. Braun found himself an object of scarcely secondary interest; if
he had had a train loaded with sawdust he could
have sold it all; and, as it was, he soon found that
he could get whatever he chose to ask for the
contents of his one wagon, and that butter had
emphatically gone up. It was long a matter of
regret with him that he had not thought to
provide himself with more 'broduce.' He parted
with the children, not without emotion, and went
back home that afternoon, bearing not only
messages from Juan and Nita, but grateful and
affectionate acknowledgments, as of a personal
service, from the Mexicans to Frau Braun. And
it should be added that Mr. Braun always found
a ready market for his wares in that town afterwards, among Americans and Mexicans alike.

As good luck would have it there was a train of *caritas* just in that morning from Mexico, loaded with bars of silver, bags of wool, hides, *frijoles*, *peloncillos*, and onions; and before the children left the plaza they were told by the major-domo that they could go back with him as soon as his cargo was sold; that he had to pass through Santa Rosa, and would gladly go out of his way a little, in order to take them all the way to the *hacienda*.

This settled, Juan and Nita were, indeed, happy; and, in the few days that intervened, everything was done that could be done to heighten and increase their happiness. It was the next best thing to being at home, to find themselves among their own people again; and, as for kindness and indulgence not even the Señora could have surpassed their new friends in devising pleasures for Juan and Nita.

The interest of the community in them had not time to flag or grow cold; and the children would certainly have been irretrievably spoiled if anything had kept them long in San Antonio. A continuous stream of Americans and Mexicans, Germans, Frenchmen, poured into the house that sheltered them. They had clothes enough sent them to have set up an orphan asylum almost, and quite a sum of money; and as for toys and sweets they were deluged with them. Nita had not the remotest idea what to do with the ten dolls sent her because she was a girl, and it was thought would be especially gratified by such a present. Juan was equally puzzled when some foolish sympathizer presented him with a pop-gun — of all things! And great was his contempt and disgust when its nature and uses were explained to him. He, with Shaneco's bow and the skill to use it; he, slayer of bears and wild-cats, to be given a pop-gun!! To tell the truth, both he and Nita were much confounded by the warmth of their reception. They could not see why it should be supposed that they had done anything remarkable.

Amigo was of a different mind. He had always known that there was something remarkable about *him;* and it was no surprise, consequently, to see his merit win the public recognition it had long deserved. He took as kindly as possible to such an agreeable state of things; and, with his usual talent for adapting himself to circumstances, now lay all day, nearly, on a straw mat near the front door, where he received all comers

with much affability at first, eating of such deli-
cacies as they offered, and submitting to endless
caresses.

It is true that this soon gave way to a polite
toleration, and then to something very like con-
temptuous indifference; but this was when his
courtesy had been severely taxed, and he had
grown weary of hearing his praises chanted in
several languages by perennial adorers. He
yawned, at last, pointedly, when anybody al-
luded to his past deeds; and never so much as
looked from under his eyebrows at any fowl, or
animal, *as food*, until it had been killed in a con-
ventional way, and cooked by the proper person,
when he partook languidly of his portion like any
other civilized being.

And you should have seen his reception of a
silver collar given him by a prominent citizen,
with 'Amigo, the Friend of Man' engraved on it
by the first jeweller of the place. Perhaps he
thought it a vulgar demonstration; perhaps he
feared that if he didn't nip such enthusiasm in the
bud he would be a sacred dog before he knew
where he was, and would be shut up in a temple,
worshipped as such for the rest of his life — a
career that would particularly bore a dog of

simple tastes and active habits; perhaps he was only out of humor. Certain it is that when the prominent citizen approached him, and, in the presence of an interested company, proceeded to decorate him as 'the Friend of Man,' he barely turned his head to see who was there; now, stretched out his neck with an air of studied indifference, yawned rudely in their faces, and sank down on his mat again without more ado, having expressed as eloquently as he could his conviction that 'the post of honor is the private station.'

During the remainder of his stay in the city he was content to pose as a mere private gentleman. It was noticed that he parted his hair in the middle all the way down his back, and only recognized such people as had the good-fortune to please him; but, somehow, he gave no offence. Everything was generously pardoned in him, and conceded to him, on the score of distinguished service in the past.

Juan and Nita were getting very restless when the major-domo suddenly appeared at their door, early one morning, and, to their great joy, announced that he was ready to start for Mexico. It would take a ream of paper to tell of all the farewells, blessings, presents, good wishes, and prayers that went with and followed the two children on this, the last stage of their long journey. Up to the very last moment something was being tucked into the *carita* for them by somebody; and, when they at last rolled off, a great number of kind hearts rejoiced to think of the great happiness that awaited the Señora, and wished them good-speed and a safe arrival with more fervor than is usually put into such speeches — their sweet, sonorous *'Adios!'* ringing in the children's ears for some time, as it was caught up and repeated on all sides. *'A Dios!'* — the last sound they had heard from their mother's lips, as she unconsciously commended them to the God who had taken them from her so suddenly, and was now so sweetly giving them back again.

After crossing the Medina and Nueces Rivers, Juan was interested to see that the game was plentiful; but, after crossing the Rio Grande, he may be said to have noticed nothing, so absorbed was he in one thought. When the children found themselves standing once more on the soil of Mexico, they were so filled with holy joy that, with the ardor of their race, they fell down on their knees and kissed the brown earth repeatedly and then, reverently crossing themselves, said an

'Our Father' and 'Hail Mary,' in thanksgiving for their safe return. Those good Catholics — their friends in San Antonio — had lost no time in recalling these prayers to their memories, so that they were able to express fittingly their devout gratitude; and then, with lightened hearts, climbed back into the *carita*, and were soon rolling slowly along again in that clumsiest of creaky vehicles.

And what of the Señora, for whom this beautiful surprise is preparing? Little dreaming of it, or only in dreams, at once consoled and tormented by an exquisite vision of it, the Señora had been steadily losing heart and hope every day and hour of these cruel years — eternities they always seemed to her afterwards. And of late a great darkness had come over her, actual and moral. Despair was settling down upon her, and the light of day as well as the light of her life would soon be gone, she thought. Constant weeping had so injured her sight that she was threatened with blindness; yet she wept on, ignorant of the harm she was doing, ever mourning for her loved and lost ones.

For some time her faith in what she firmly believed to be an apparition (lovingly vouchsafed

her) of the Madonna buoyed her up so strongly
that she had not only borne the silence and
emptiness of her life with some courage, but had
occupied herself in planning and working out
certain things in view of the children's return.
But, as time went on, all this was given up. For
two years she put by a certain sum of money
after the sheep-shearing was over, with which to
buy for her darlings whatever should be needed
when they came back. In the third year she
added to it, and said to herself, '*If* they ever
come back they will want a great many things,'
and often counted the hoarded store. It seemed
to make their return a real and possible thing for
the time being, and was the only thing that gave
her any pleasure. But, when the summer of the
fourth year came, she thought despairingly,
'They will never come, perhaps.'

She could not bear to feel that it was quite
settled even then; but she practically renounced
the precious hope; for when the Nativity of the
Blessed Virgin came around, on the eighth of
September, she took the whole sum, and put it
into a purse that had belonged to her husband,
and carried it to Santa Rosa, where, after many
prayers before the high altar, and groans that

could not be uttered, she gave it to the Church; and, if some earthly dross mingled with the gold, some yearning hope that Heaven even now might be moved by such a splendid gift to have mercy upon a heart-broken woman, and restore her children, I am sure it was forgiven to this simple soul, for 'she loved much.'

On the evening of that day, at sunset, the major-domo's train was winding across the plain toward the *hacienda*. Unable to bear the slowness of its progress Juan and Nita leaped out of the *carita* and ran along ahead. Presently they came to the very place where they had been captured. There was the plain on which the flocks had been pastured that day; there was the lake still glittering in the sun; the trees under which they had sat with their father. How well they remembered it all! And then their eyes fell upon a heap of stones which, with a rude cross, marked their father's grave. They looked at it with tears in their eyes; but they were now very near home, and were drawn to it by every sweet and powerful influence.

They quickened their pace to the utmost, they arrived at the gate of the *hacienda*. Juan tore it open, and they rushed across the courtyard and threw themselves upon a lady who was walking there with her *reboso* drawn close around her face and her dim eyes fixed sadly upon the setting sun!

The Señora, who had her back to them, felt herself suddenly seized from the rear, arms were flung about her, voices shrieked out, '*Madre! Madre! Mi Madre!*' Her heart gave a wild thrill, at hearing herself called 'mother' again. Turning she found herself in the grasp of two strangers. She had kept the image of her children as they looked when she last saw them. Oh, how fondly, miserably, constantly, she had dwelt upon it! She did not at first recognize them in these tall, rough, dark creatures. She strained her eyes to see them more clearly, and put forth her trembling hands to feel them.

Just then Amigo bounded up to her and leaped upon her. *He* had not changed, and she knew the truth. Was it a sob or a shriek that she gave as her knees gave way under her, and, clutching her children frantically to her breast, she fell upon her knees? There, the mother and children stayed, clinging, clinging to each other, weeping out the sting of their long separation, covering each other with kisses, only the sweeter for being so long

denied, delirious with joy — a sight to make men
and angels glad.

. . . .

And now old Santiago came hobbling around
the house, and the major-domo was at the gate,
and the herders, and the women about the place
caught scent of what was happening, and now
there were shrieks and tears, and laughter, and a
Babel of confusion and talk, if you will! And, in
the midst of it all, the Señora turned faint, and
had to go indoors, leaning on Juan, who was on
one side of her, and on Nita, who was on the
other, and murmuring brokenly, 'I am content to
die now. I have seen my children again.' And
now the major-domo had to take himself off,
after being overwhelmed with thanks. And now
the servants hurried inside. And now the sun
dropped out of sight. The day of burning heat
and cruel grief was over, and night had come to
heal and restore and bind up, with influences
sweeter than any Job found in the Pleiades, the
wounds that had been inflicted four years before.

By the time the lights had been lit in the
hacienda all the neighborhood was astir. Old
Martina ran all the way from her *jacal* when she
heard the glorious news, as though she had been

a girl of fifteen, and disappeared inside a door that received every relative she had in the course of the next hour.

Except in heaven there was never such rejoicing. It is not too much to say that the whole population of Santa Rosa lived at the *hacienda* for a month in detachments of from three to a dozen people, and the wonderful story was repeated in an ever-widening circle, until it actually reached the ears of the President himself, who sent the Señora a beautiful letter of congratulation.

Amigo's behavior was just what might have been expected. The Señora, after spending the greater part of the night on her knees before her crucifix, went outside next morning, to get some fresh air, and tranquillize her mind a little, and there, curled up in the very spot that he had long ago marked for his own, was Amigo. There was a very pretty and affectionate interview between them; and Amigo certainly had no reason to complain of the Señora's coldness now. He was, doubtless, much affected by her kindness, and vowed renewed loyalty to her and hers; for, that evening, he quietly resumed his old duties; brought in a strange flock for the first time, and, in two weeks, knew every goat, sheep, and lamb among them.

There is a new *adobe* wall around the *hacienda* now; the Señora's oleanders are in bloom, and perfume the whole garden, which is in charming order, and has all sorts of new flowers in it. Shaneco's bow, and Amigo's pack-saddle hang on the walls of the Señora's room, which also boasts a new statue of the Blessed Virgin, before which a light burns continually. Juan has taken charge of his father's property, and is now more entirely his mother's staff than ever, and the Señora, with Juanita's help, bakes *tortillas* and *pan de gloria*, spins yarn, and weaves *serapes*, but no longer weeps.

THE END